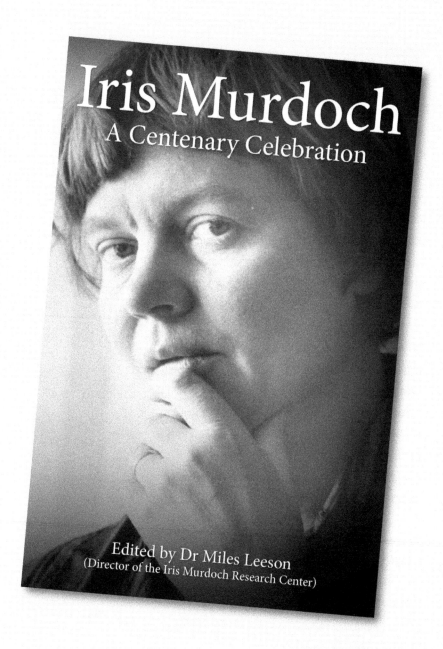

Iris Murdoch
A Centenary Celebration

Edited by Dr Miles Leeson
(Director of the Iris Murdoch Research Center)

Iris Murdoch: A Centenary Celebration
Edited by Miles Leeson

Miles Leeson has asserted the
moral right to be identified as author of this work.
Designed and typeset by Ian Bayley.
British Library Cataloguing in Publication Data
A catalogue record for this book is available from the
British Library
Published by Sabrestorm Fiction, The Olive Branch,
Caen Hill, Devizes, Wiltshire SN10 1RB United Kingdom.

Website: www.sabrestormfiction.com
Email: books@sabrestormfiction.com

ISBN 9781912972005

For Iris, with love

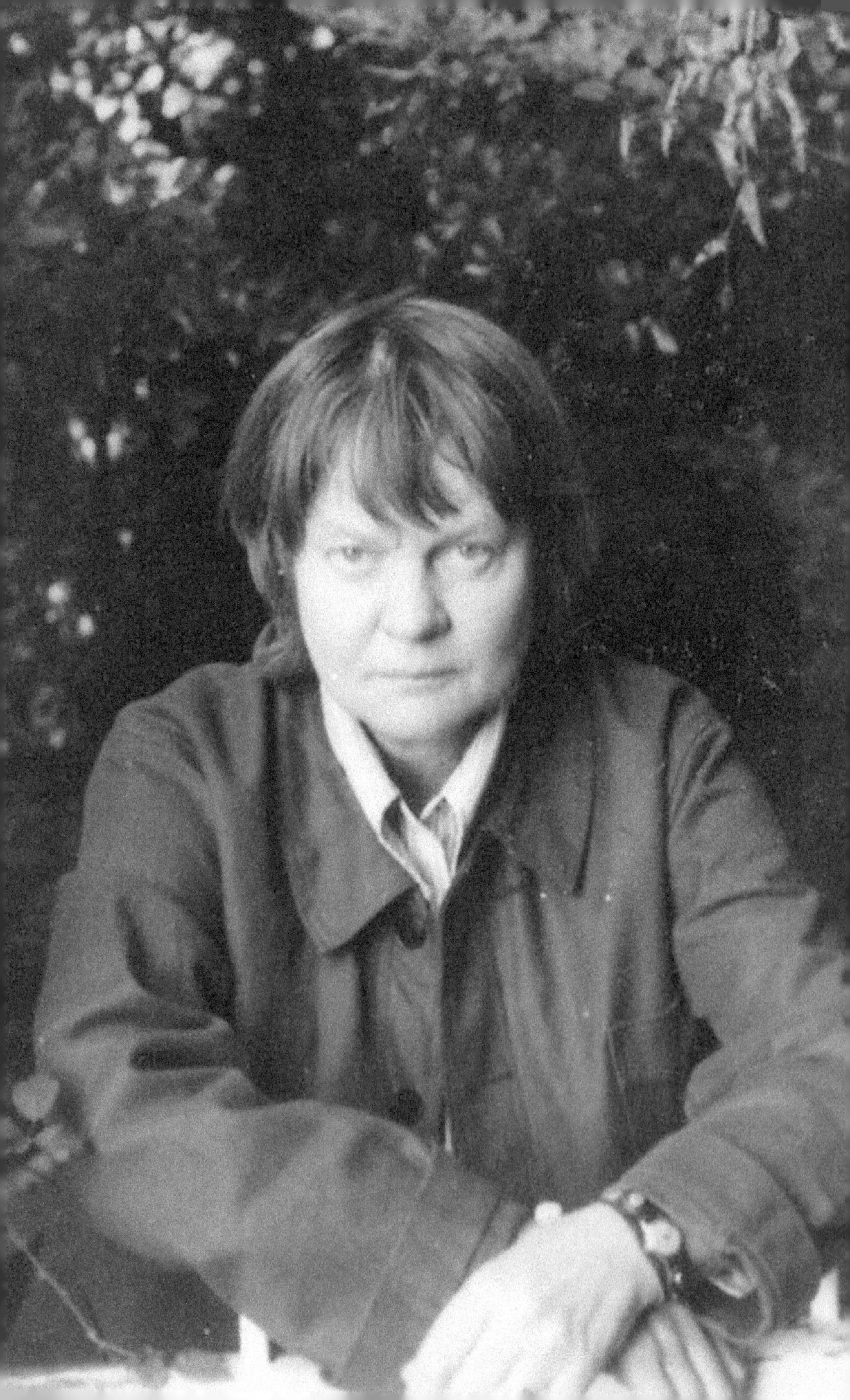

CONTENTS

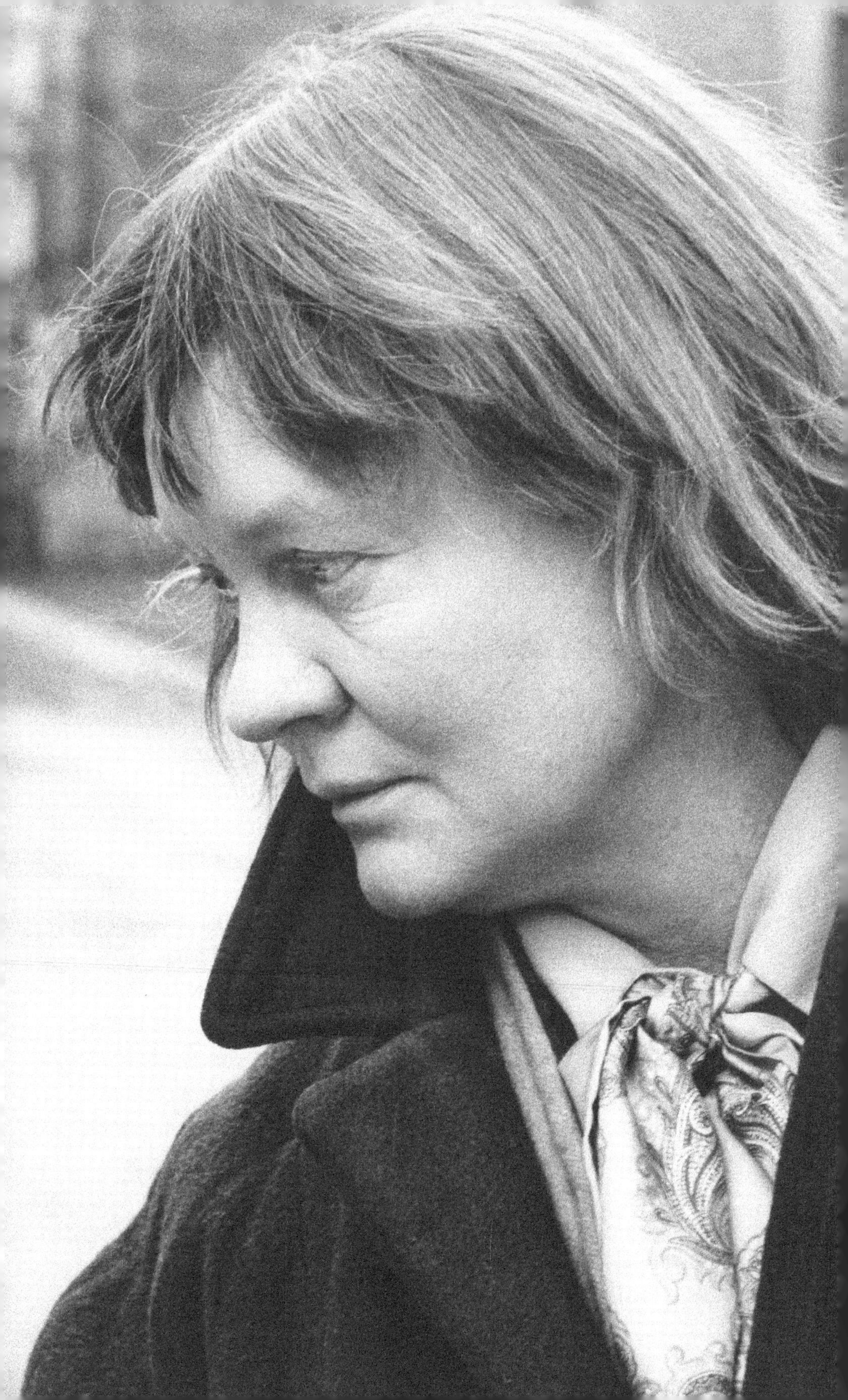

Preface

Iris Murdoch's life and work will probably be familiar to readers of this volume. Although her fictional work suffered in popularity (and in sales) after her death in 1999 it is now, quite rightly, undergoing a renaissance: this follows on from the developing interest in her philosophy over the last ten years. Her centenary year then, twenty years after she left us, is not only a celebration of her life, but looks forward to the continuing academic and popular interest in her not only as an author but as a thinker. The enduring image of her since 2001 as a victim of Alzheimer's is now, at last, giving way to one focused on the body of her work.

Due to her prolific letter writing, collected in the wonderful *Living on Paper: Letters from Iris Murdoch 1934-1995*, and, of course, the biographies by Bayley, Conradi, White, and Wilson, she is one of the most well-known public figures of the last century. But what was she really like in private? This collection, by turns informative, comedic, and poignant, fills in the gaps in the biographies and letters; we see a multifaceted, playful, witty, travel-loving confidante who, above all, loved company and bringing joy to others. Her friends, fellow students, colleagues, past students, and professional contacts all attest to her great strengths, and the care and love they received from her. I am delighted to include a full transcript, as a coda to the collection, of an interview I conducted with A.N. Wilson at the Eighth Iris Murdoch Biennial Conference at Chichester in September 2017. Andrew Wilson reflects on his own biographical work and concludes that 'If I were to write it now, I would entitle it Iris Murdoch: As I Didn't Know Her'. A wide-ranging life, and one that is reflected in the diversity of her own fictional work.

The collection was started by Peter J. Conradi, to whom we owe the deepest debt, in expectation of her eigthtieth birthday. As she died in the February of her 80th year, the materials were presented to the Archives at

Kingston University by Peter Conradi along with his archives relating to *Iris Murdoch: A Life* and have remained untouched since. At the suggestion of the former director of the Centre for Iris Murdoch Studies at Kingston, Anne Rowe (now Visiting Professor at the University of Chichester), the process of sifting and editing this material was begun in 2017 in order for this collection to come together. This was aided by Frances White, deputy director of the Centre here, and by Heather Robbins who undertook so much of the transcription. Those three have been a constant support. I am also grateful to Ian Beck for the kind permission to reproduce photographs taken by Iris' close friend Janet Stone. Ian has been a long-time supporter of the Iris Murdoch Society and I am delighted that images by his late mother-in-law illustrate the collection.

Although this collection is, quite rightly, dedicated to Iris, it is for her dedicated readers, those new to her work, those who will discover her in years to come – and to my students who continue to inspire my own work.

Miles Leeson
University of Chichester, June 2019

A lifelong Friendship

Dame Philippa Foot

Iris and I were at Somerville together, though I hardly knew her then. She, reading Classical Mods and Greats, had come up before the War, whereas I, in three-year Philosophy, Politics and Economics, arrived only in 1939. But we both left in 1942, and our friendship began that summer when, told by Donald MacKinnon that I was ill and struggling with Finals, she came to my lodgings with a bunch of flowers. We had each of us been taught by MacKinnon, who was soon to be a great influence on our lives, but as he was nearly thirty, we were apt to think of him then as if he were a prophet with a beard, being astonished years later to find how close in age he was to us.

After Finals Iris disappeared to work in London while I worked in Oxford, and we saw little of each other until I got a job in London in 1943 and went to stay with her in 5 Seaforth Place, which is an alley way running off Buckingham Gate. I meant to find a place of my own, which indeed I did; but as Iris said she supposed that we would in future spend half the week in her flat and half the week in mine it struck us that one flat would be better than two, and I stayed on in that strange series of open 'rooms,' then above a warehouse, but earlier having been a storage area with stables down below.

Let me try to give a picture of our life in 'Seaforth' as we always called it, its number being rather notional as it was the alley way's only front door.

First of all, the fact that it was war time dominated the scene. The worst of the bombing of the City was over, but even before the terrifying advent of the flying VI and V2 bombs, there were many air raids and people from the devastated East End were sleeping in bunks on the platforms of the tube stations, trekking in to central London each night and out to work in the mornings. Strangers sheltering in doorways would sometimes accompany each other home until the last of us had to go home alone. Iris and I suffered only a window blown in one morning, finding the alarm clock officious when it went off five minutes later! But alone in the flat one or other of us might sleep for shelter in the bath tub under the stairs, kept awake by discomfort and the magnified sound of rats who seemed to be scrabbling at its sides.

Life was spartan in Seaforth. The blackout for the skylight doubled as a bed covering, so that I was instructed on my first night there to pull it down over me once the lights were out; and when the weather was really cold we would put on our overcoats over our clothes before we got into bed. In the day time, an ancient gas fire, which was the only heating, gave us a few pale inches of wartime gas. Mercifully there was always enough coming through the equally ancient gas cooker to allow us to take hot water bottles to bed, but, of course, in the end rubber bottles were no more and unyielding stone things had to take their place. Hot water bottles have appeared quite often in Iris' novels and I am not surprised.

Then, of course, there were the food shortages, mitigated for us by the fact that a Lyons tea shop across Victoria Street gave us not only breakfast warmth but tea or coffee and sticky buns. Sometimes, though I think it cannot have been very often, we ate in pleasant restaurants in Charlotte Street or in other Soho haunts, while older, richer friends like Thomas Balogh or Nickie Kaldor would take us out expecting to pay for the meal, as men at that time usually did. The five shilling limit on restaurant meals which did a lot for social justice in a time of strict rationing was, in any case, in force. I do not remember that Iris and I felt poor: the problem was to find the things that one really needed in the shops.

Clothes rationing did not, I think, worry us much. But the fact that we had only three pairs of shoes for the two of us was troublesome given the amount of walking that had to be done. When Iris' one pair was being mended she had to wear a pair of mine, and I remember bitterly complaining that I got them back as 'flat bottom boats,' which was what they were called from that time on. In a way, however, it was odd how much life went on in spite of the strange conditions. We would walk across London to parties, and stand waiting for the last underground train home in front of the East End families already bedded down for the night. We even gave one or two parties at Seaforth, and I only wish I could remember more of the people who came. There must have been poets and others who Iris had asked but I remember only Tambimuttu, the editor of a current poetry review. On my side there was my sister Marion and cousin Rosalind. And there were people like Tommy and Nickie, originally my friends, but now very much Iris' too. Stevie Smith used to come, and I think Jane Degras, through whom I knew Stevie, and the ex-burglar and author, Mark Benny, who lived with Jane.

My memories of the years that Iris and I lived together in such amity are full of laughter and many small jokes. We were, after all, still young and ready for silliness, as when we decided to tell each other of the men who had asked us to marry them. My so called 'list' was soon done, and as Iris' went on and on I suggested crossly that it would be quicker if she told me of the ones who hadn't asked her rather than those who had. But of course there was anguish too, not only about our love affairs, but about men who were away at the war. On one terrible day, alerted by Donald MacKinnon, I had to go back to Seaforth to tell Iris that Frank Thompson, whom she loved dearly, had been taken prisoner with an ill-fated Partisan group in Bulgaria, and shot by allies of the Germans in cold blood.

What was Iris like in those days? She was serious and orderly, sitting down to read the moment she came in to the flat and tidying things away if I left them out. Already she had written a novel about which, sadly, I remember practically nothing, except that it was set in London and contained a character called Stuart! There was never any doubt but that she would do something extraordinary later on, and she did not dissent when I said that she had, as I did not, an entry in an imaginary diary reading 'Mem. To make my mark.'

Above all there was a magic about Iris, generally felt, and by women as well as by many men. The magic had, I think, much to do with the way she combined reserve and spontaneity. Obviously she lived deeply within herself; and yet she was completely present, a wonderful listener and apt to ask questions that made others seem more interesting to themselves. Absolutely loyal to her oldest friends through all her years of fame, she aroused great devotion in them. It may seem a strange idea, but the thought sometimes comes to me that for all the delights of her novels, and the interest of her philosophical works, she herself was better than they are.

Undergraduates Together

Roy Jenkins

I first knew Iris Murdoch in that curious half-light of 'the Phony War', which lasted over the autumn, winter and early spring of 1939-40 until it was abruptly ended by German troops sweeping into the Low Countries and France on May 10th. We were both undergraduates, she at Somerville and I at Balliol, with the war, 'phony' or otherwise, making at that stage, surprisingly little physical impact upon the majority who remained for the time being at Oxford, although with a future of more active engagement looming more or less closely.

We were also both very politically engaged, although by no means from identical standpoints, and not in a way conducive to a particularly amicable relationship. The Oxford University Labour Club had in the last years of the peace managed to contain in tolerable harmony a mixture of Communists and Social Democrats. The latter were mostly well to the left of the official Labour party line as expounded by Attlee, Morrison and Dalton. And the Communists were in a 'popular front' phase, with emphasis on a common resistance to fascism abroad and to Chamberlain at home. The Nazi-Soviet pact in August, 1939 and the outbreak of war a week or so later changed all that. Moscow's reversal of alliance meant that what might a short time before have been described as a 'people's struggle' (and again became so after the German invasion of Russia in June, 1941) turned temporarily into an 'imperialist war'. This made life very uncomfortable within the nominally united club, particularly for the Social Democrats, as the Communists appeared to be in the majority; they at least had the executive committee under firm control. The position was exacerbated when the Soviet army invaded Finland at the end of the year.

As a result Anthony Crosland, I and the one other Social Democrat on the executive committee, when we came back from the Easter vacation of 1940, and thinking ourselves very bold, split the increasingly unco-ordinated pantomime horse and set up, under a somewhat turgid title, the O.U. Democratic Socialist Club. We then had all the initial success, and rapidly became the bigger of the two halves. But Iris Murdoch, who had never been a camp follower of easy success, remained, strange though it may seem today, apparently rigid on the Stalinist line. Perhaps she just disliked us. At any rate she did not come. But nor for that matter did such subsequently major and not notably left-wing figures as Denis Healey and Leo Pliatzky, the Treasury knight of the 1970s who invented the best formula for a rigid control of public expenditure.

Iris was therefore in quite good company, but what was of more interest from the point of view of our relations was that she was Treasurer of the old Labour Club, which retained title and legitimacy, and that I was Treasurer of the new upstart organisation. As a result we engaged in a long and unrewarding correspondence about the sharing of the minuscule assets (or liabilities, which were probably greater, hence the concern) of the old club. Both our different ideological positions and the arm's-length nature of our negotiations were indicated by our respective salutations, 'Dear Comrade Jenkins', her letters began – I was surprised that she did not excommunicate me from the category. 'Dear Miss Murdoch' I formally and coolly replied. All this, I fear, took place while the British Expeditionary Force was retreating to Dunkirk and the German armies were racing across the fields of Picardy. Student politics have rarely been notable for their sense of proportion.

It was sixteen years later before she came back into my consciousness. Despite reading that it was a worthy successor to Joyce Cary's *The Horse's Mouth* (I was not in any event a great fan of Cary) I did not read either her first novel *Under the Net* (1954) or *The Flight from the Enchanter* (1955). But I was captivated by *The Sandcastle* (1957) and from then on read and for a quarter of a century after that read almost all her novels as they appeared. I particularly remember *The Bell, An Unofficial Rose, The Black Prince, The Sea, The Sea* and *The Philosopher's Pupil*. And of these the most vivid impact was made by the end of *The Sea, The Sea*. As I wrote in my diary which I then kept for January 11th, 1979 when, as President of the European Commission, I was on an official visit to Ghana: 'I then spent two late-night hours finishing The Sea, The Sea, feeling that the combined effect of staying in this rather gimcrack State House in this steaming, rundown country and Iris Murdoch's phantasmagoria were having a distinctly unsettling effect on me'.

Well into this period I buttressed literary admiration with personal friendship. The link, I think was reforged in 1979 when we spent a week together staying in the house of John and Patsy Grigg in Catalonia. Thereafter we had family luncheons, either at East Hendred or in the enchanting chaos of Steeple Acton and later in the more constrained (and therefore marginally less chaotic) circumstances of North Oxford. The Bayleys' houses always provided exceptionally long, hilarious and well-lubricated luncheon parties. This phase culminated, although happily did not end, in my giving Iris an Oxford honorary degree on my inaugural (and therefore personally chosen) list as Chancellor. That gave me particular pleasure, for not only had her work richly earned it, but I felt that, forty-seven year later, it was achieving a higher balance than our ungracious 1940 correspondence had attained.

Iris as Mentor

Marjorie Boulton

When I went up to Somerville in October, 1941, to read English, I was younger than the usual student, and probably even pathetically naive, coming from a small grammar school in North Lincolnshire. I was poorer than most students and had a strong northern/midland accent which was not an advantage. Yet Iris gave me a remarkable friendship which was one of the great generosities to impinge upon my life.

I met her in the context of Oxford political life which I began as a member of the Democratic Socialist Club (Labour Party) and she was already a member of the Labour Club (more, or less Communist; she was a member of the Party at that time). I suspect now that all of us took student politics a great deal too seriously, but in Oxford such societies did get outstanding speakers and we felt important. I have the impression that even then, fervent though Iris was, there was some element in her of self-irony and distrust of dramatization – against which she on occasion warned me. She was then in her final year, reading Greats and enjoyed the luxury of a room in the main house, with easy access to the dining-room, common-room, etc. She was thus very visible, and my early recollection is of her rather swinging up and down, with a purposeful look, and her shortish blonde hair bouncing as she walked.

Even then I got a very strong impression of a real personality, strongly individual, yet, I think, without any forced attempt, so common in Oxford, to be a Personality – no hint of self-dramatization, affectation, or setting out to be interesting. And yet she already radiated power. Something of this quiet, modest charisma was felt by quite a group of left-wing Somervillians, most of them much more self-confident than I was; I think we all felt it a privilege to get into conversation with her.

At Somerville, while there was no severe etiquette, students in one year group did not mix much with others, but Iris was friendly to her juniors and often kind and helpful. A very impressive memory is of what I believe was actually the evening before she started Finals, certainly very late before them: she had agreed to give a talk to some of us left-wing students, and gave a very illuminating talk on the political poets of the Thirties: MacNeice, Auden, Spender, Day-Lewis, etc. I was astounded by her range of knowledge and her excellent reading. Another door opened for me, never to close again. At that time she wrote some poetry herself – at least once read some to me – it all seemed to me brilliant and advanced and exciting, but she herself felt it immature – it takes a very developed mind to be so conscious of its limitations!

I believe that already she had, in addition to her knowledge of the classics, a very wide knowledge of British and European literature, and a wide range of general information. Of course to me she was dazzlingly sophisticated; and, painfully naive though I was, I was already bright enough to see her knowledge of the world as much more impressive than the louder sophistication of some of the students whose talk was more posh and who wore elaborate and expensive make-up and had somehow got hold of smart clothes. I do not think that at any time in my relationship with Iris did I see her doing anything that could be called showing off; indeed, I would say that she was essentially a humble person and certainly very unaffected. (Most of my experience has been that people who really are important seldom feel an urge to push to make themselves so!) And yet she went about in a blazing light of specialness of which she seemed unaware. Admiring remarks were dismissed affectionately but firmly.

I went up to Oxford, in my father's phrase, 'an undenominational Christian' and moved away from religion partly as a result of reading Marxist literature, but probably even more as a result of angry encounters with young Anglicans and various aspects of narrow sectarianism; I had tried also to learn by attending a wide range of services, ranging from Russian Orthodox to Christian Science. I do not now remember how far I discussed such matters with Iris, but I do remember that, however much she must have found me naive and ignorant, she always showed a kind of respect for my muddled religion – part of her general respect for other people's experience and endeavours. I think now that her tolerance was an aspect of her integrity even more than of her good manners. But to her I must often have seemed almost a peasant!

Many of us missed her very much when she left after Finals.
I remember how delighted I was (though I ought not to have felt any
surprise!) when in my father's *Times Educational Supplement* I saw that she
had obtained a First.

Iris went to work with the Civil Service, about which she sometimes
wrote to me amusingly. She had her little flat in Seaforth Place, and I was
actually invited to visit her there. Again, this was a revelation to me of a
lifestyle almost exotic. I remember noticing the range (and the value!) of
the books she already had. I believe she abandoned her decent bed to me
and herself slept in a camp bed, on my infrequent visits. She was very kind
in all sorts of details. I still remember how she took me out to supper in a
Soho restaurant and never showed any sign of irritation or scorn because I
was so bewildered! I remember how on one occasion in her flat in Seaforth
Place she did encourage me to talk a bit about a love-problem I had at
that time; she was very kind, very patient, and helped me a lot by asking
intelligent questions.

A characteristic which I find admirable, which I observed at a very early
stage in our friendship, was her warmth of manner; she was not afraid of
affectionate gestures: she would put her arm round someone, pat someone,
give a hug; and I believe later in life she did say, for example to the young
scholar-poet Andrew Harvey, that we ought to hug one another rather
more. Interesting in a generation that was often educated to be very
inhibited about friendly caresses, and often exaggeratedly suspicious of
them or even disgusted by them. She knew the reassurance and comfort
of a bit of non-sexual bodily affectionateness. (I never thought she had
any lesbian inclinations and I do not remember hearing anyone else
wondering.) Of course her warm and often comforting or reassuring
manner did not blunt any intellectual or moral integrity. I suppose her
essential values were Truth and Love, and she knew that one without the
other could be inadequate.

A gift she had from an early age but developed very much as she became
famous (and, presumably, had a lot of often tiresome fan mail) was one I
have still not acquired: she could write a letter of only a few lines which
immediately gave the recipient a real sense of her kindness and her interest
in the other person. And yet, in contrast, she could take the trouble to find
a postcard or greeting card that suited the recipient or the situation, and

perhaps adorn it with some daft little sketch – often as deft as it was daft – and several colours of ink.

I believe Iris was somewhat angry, not with me, when, after several short-list interviews for junior university posts, I accepted a former tutor's advice to give up this quest and be content with something inferior. Much later in life Iris remembered, this and had some fairly strong comments on it, believing, I think, that a certain snobbery had played a part in the advice.

I plodded on in teacher training and with some very minor authorship; she soared and deserved everything; and I did very much hesitate to intrude upon her. Unless my memory deceives me, we really resumed close relations only when in 1971 I returned to Oxford, to do a D.Phil after the collapse of my second-rate career in 1970. At some time in the intervening period, a friend helped me to get (before this was a simple matter) adequate contraceptive information, and I understand that it was Iris who found out for herself and then her friends: a part of her regard for other people's freedom. I made friends with someone else in London, whose life had been largely unlucky, but who had been in Iris' large circle of friends. For Various reasons, though she took an Oxford degree (and, I believe, never technically received it because she could not afford to return for the ceremony) she was poor and underprivileged, a victim in more ways than one. She once confided in me that when she accidentally and in her rather squalid circumstances became pregnant, disastrously, it was Iris who, in those illiberal days, managed to arrange a proper surgical abortion for her – and paid for it. Her gratitude lasted, I believe, a lifetime.

For some time she and John had a lovely rambling old house in Steeple Aston; I remember visiting her there and being impressed by the wealth of interesting ornaments, paintings, etc., Iris' own study in which her books were written (still with a pen), the huge numbers of books indicating the breadth of her culture as well as for specialist professional concerns – and almost equally impressed by the anarchic disorganisation of the kitchen and to some extent other rooms. Iris had more important things to do than be a housewife; and, though she could afford some domestic help, I believe she was not very good at firmly ordering other people about.

When I was principal of the Charlotte Mason College of Education, Iris, I think in 1963 or 1964, agreed to come to Westmorland (now Cumbria), so very much indeed out of her way to make the star speech at the college Open Day. My deputy principal was an unhappy, embittered woman who had had a deal of genuine bad luck in life and combined great ability and industry with a personality that could at times be perplexing. When she learned that the distinguished writer was to come to the small college, she told me almost aggressively that she was not interested in important people, she would not treat Iris Murdoch any differently from anyone else, I must not expect any deference from her, whatever others did, and so on. Someone like that wasn't anything special and she was not going to make up to her.

Iris came; was instantly polite and friendly to everyone; and gave a very good talk to the students and guests, not above their heads, not pretentious, but direct and sincere; as far as I remember, about the value of reading and knowledge. it was almost comical to see how her charm, her kindness and especially this gift of hers for finding other people interesting, overcame my deputy principal, who finished up enchanted with her and never lost interest in her until a tragic last long illness destroyed her memory. Later, she occasionally dropped my colleague a few kind words. Eventually we both went to see her at Steeple Aston, a happy and successful visit. I have a special memory of her kindness to this ill-starred woman: she had an idea of writing a novel. Now, this novel was based in part on her experiences of the college, and when it was complete I recognised a revenge element in it, even to some extent against myself. Privately published, it was not very good, but she could have written quite a good novel if she had thought more about technique, and more about readers, less about vengeance; she did have some ability for narrative and dialogue, plot and good plain English.

Her own creative work was, of course, hugely important to her – as such a part of our lives should be – and relatively late in our careers we visited Steeple Aston together again and Iris agreed to see her first chapter. It was not, I emphasise, stupid work; there was genuine promise there; but it was moving and impressive to see how Iris noticed good points, took my friend absolutely seriously, encouraged her, treated her as interesting; an experience which, after many embittering experiences, did her a great deal of good. The impression of Iris' graciousness and encouragement remained with her for a long time, and did a little to counter some of the insults she had suffered in other quarters.

When I was working for my D.Phil. (1971 onwards), on Charles Reade, Iris did me an enormous favour, letting me stay free of charge in her London flat for I think a little over a month, so that I could study Reade's 80+ notebooks in the London Library – I could not have afforded accommodation in London, and the use of the flat also meant that I could prepare cheap meals for myself. I also learned, partly from evidence visible, that other friends had borrowed her flat and some had also rather exploited her goodness – I can at least claim that I was the one who learned where to put the rubbish out that several must have left. I did all I could to clean up and put small things right, and Iris and John were very pleased to see this, but alas, in trying to stand on a chair to clean a window, I broke an old chair I did not know was a Chippendale. This was forgiven, and all I could do was write a Shakespearian parody by way of atonement. (In fairness to myself, a chair that falls into splinters when stood on cannot be in mint condition to start with!) But I shall not forget how, Iris lent me and many others her expensive flat, and trusted us; and told me comfortingly that 'everybody breaks something'. She helped all sorts of people in distress.

A merit in Iris which I sometimes wished she had a little less of unlike almost everyone, was her reluctance to talk about herself, especially about her work. I longed to hear more about her writing and her successes, and about her many adventures abroad, but it was very difficult to get anything out of her that was about Iris Murdoch! She had this wonderful social, and more than social, gift for making other people feel that they were interesting to her; always a great and often a difficult courtesy; but I believe that often they really were.

In a culture which I suspect lays too much emphasis for women (and, I believe, increasingly for men) on dress, coiffure and cosmetics, and in which we are – encouraged to worry about our appearance far beyond mere hygiene and tidiness, I should think Iris had about as little physical vanity as any woman could have. I never saw evidence that she was interested in dresses, I doubt if she often wore make-up and her very casual hairstyle looked almost neglected but also looked right for her. A chic Iris would have been a gilded lily.

Sometimes she wore a piece of jewellery that was a most unusual curiosity from her travels – perhaps a Buddhist emblem or some odd souvenir – she must have liked meaning rather than glamour. Similarly, I do not think she cared much about the look of her homes; but she liked many personal treasures of curious objects and interesting works of art, no room in which I ever saw her was anything like a page from a women's magazine!

Her final illness was, of course, appalling, and hideously ironical, when a powerful intellect and a brilliant creativity were destroyed by mere physical failure as the cells died in her brain. Towards the end I longed to be some use to her and could not, except that, not often (I think about once a month), she could come to lunch at my home, eat, drink and pet my cats, and John could safely leave her with me, knowing that she knew me and would be cared for. The last time she came, it became all too clear that she could no longer be entrusted to me, as she panicked at the absence of John; the couple would have been still welcome, but in fact this was the last time I saw her. At least with me she had a poor appetite and tended to forget to eat. What, however, I remember most touchingly of the last terrible months is that for a long time after the end of intellect and the failure of short-term memory, she would ask me most affectionately (if, of course, very repetitively) whether I had lately been on some foreign trip, what I had seen, had I done something exciting? She had, then, some dim idea still of who I was, but, most of all, some love remained; she was still asking someone else about themselves, not talking about herself. In this generosity of heart, at least, she may be said to have very nearly died as she had lived.

The Saintly Iris

Pierre Riches

The first thing that I remember seeing is the back of Iris' neck – but the actual nape was hidden by those long strands of blonde hair; I had noticed her very characteristic voice, and, when she turned, her stifling, taut features. It was in Cambridge and it must have been in 1947, and we were probably both listening to John Wisdom lecturing to Moral Sciences undergraduates.

A few days later I was having dinner with a friend of mine, Elisabeth Sewell, the novelist, and told her I thought this Iris woman had an interesting face – and voice. Elisabeth knew her and said she would have us to dinner together. And so a long and delightful friendship between Iris and me began.

A few months later, in the summer of '48 if my dates are correct, Iris decided to join me in Italy, and we were to go to Rome together; both of us on our first visit there. I was in Italy travelling with Jean-Francois Bergery, another Cambridge friend of mine, a rather exotic figure whom Iris much liked (she had a great weakness for exotic figures). Jean-Francois' father had been Vichy Ambassador to Ankara – a very important post during the war –, but his parents had divorced, and his mother had later married Emanuel d'Astier de la Vigerie, a French Resistance fighter who was one of de Gaulle's ministers immediately after the war. D'Astier and Louha had a lovely flat on the top floor, overlooking the Seine, at 1, Quai aux Fleurs, on l'Isle de la Cite'. And that is where I stayed, with Jean-Francois, on my first trips to Paris.

This is the sort of background Iris loves, and she thought that with all our strange backgrounds, Jean-Francois and I were the right sort to be together. That summer I travelled in Italy with Jean-Francois, and in

Florence Iris joined us. I still have a photo taken by me of both of them walking down a Florence street. Abandoning Jean-Francois, Iris and I went off to Rome by train. On the way, we discussed where we should stay. Iris told me that she had asked Fraenkel, the Oxford classicist where he advised her to go, and he had suggested the Santa Chiara next to the Piazza della Minerva.

And it is there that we stayed. The hotel still exists, though it has been refurbished and has lost some of its charm. Iris would get up early and roam around Rome before the Museums opened. She thought – rightly – that that was an excellent time to see the city and visit the churches where the faithful were often still at Mass. I sometimes joined her then, but more often we'd meet for breakfast a bit later in the morning.

One or two summers later Iris joined me in Milan. I was living there at the time, wondering what I would do next, and my father who also lived there, was very anxious that I should join him in his business. He was also anxious that I should have a girlfriend, as he had heard rumours about my wanting to become a Catholic, though I do not think he yet imagined that I might want to become a Priest.

Anyhow, Iris came visiting, and stayed with Franca Magistretti – an interesting woman, who had just started to teach psychology at the University of the Sacred Heart in Milan. She was later to become a nun, and Mother Superior – which she still is – of the female section of the religious order founded by Giuseppe Dossetti.

Franca and Iris got on extremely well, and I think that they wrote to each other for some time, but it was my father who spoilt Iris. He bought her a pullover and moccasins, which at the time (early '50's) were 'new', and all the rage in Italy. He was very fastidious, and secretly disapproved of Iris' habit of going around in sandals. For many years, Iris reminded me of those gifts of my father, particularly of the shoes which were of excellent quality. She liked them very much, and used them for a long time.

Soon after that I was baptised a Catholic and did not see Iris for a few years. I had the feeling that she was not very happy at what I had done. I can't remember when I next saw her, it must have been in the late fifties, and by then I was a Priest, or well on my way to becoming one.

I remember clearly, that we met in a pub in London, and after about 10 minutes conversation – catching up – Iris said tame very surprised: 'but you have not changed at all'. I, in turn, was greatly surprised that she had thought I would have changed that much, and then understood her reticence regarding my conversion. That 'not changing' re-established our old relationship, and since then, whenever I went to England we at least talked on the phone, and more often than not met for lunch in a pub in London or at her house, or at the Mitre in Oxford.

I was in England in 1976 and was travelling North from London. I wanted to see quite a few friends who lived in different parts of the country. The arrangement was that I would stay with some friend, and my next host would pick me up from there. I decided to go to Oxford by train, see Iris, and be picked up there in the afternoon to go to my next stop. I had heard that Iris was not well, but I understood that she was well enough to see me. I telephoned, and there was no difficulty talking to her, and we arranged that I should go to her house, have lunch, and be picked up in the early afternoon. When I arrived, she seemed much as usual, very affectionate though perhaps less ebullient and slightly dishevelled. Her eyes were not as intense as usual, nor as penetrating.

She gave me a pleasant sandwich lunch – toasted cheese – and conversation was more of the reminiscing sort than the thinking and Iris-questioning sort. (Iris always asked very direct and forthright questions, which were saved from being indiscreet only because of her natural kindness and caring. She knew very well when a question might be embarrassing. But she went as far as she could without being embarrassing).

Then I asked her to sign her last book for me (I have an almost complete collection of Iris' books signed – one, I think is missing). It was then that I was pained. Iris said: 'I always forget how you spell your name?' (she had written it hundreds of times).

'Pierre,' I said, 'not Pier as the Italians do'. And she wrote it. But obviously there was something unpleasantly obscure happening to her.

Except for a few years in the mid-fifties, Iris was the sort of friend – and fortunately, I have many of them – who have been very close to you at some stage, but whom the circumstances of life – mostly distance – have separated you from. The strong friendship remains, and a phone call, a letter, a meeting, revives the friendship; in a very few minutes everything is as it was at the best of times. There is a trust, a confidence, which neither time nor distance impairs.

In Cambridge 50 or so years ago, Iris expressed it to me by saying (and this is one of the many things she taught me): 'You can do no wrong for me' meaning that trust was there permanently. This, of course, is the love of friendship – for St. Thomas Aquinas, the highest form of love – where there is understanding and where one knows excuses will be found if there are any at all to find,

She also taught me that love is not like a cake which you distribute, and at the end, there is no more cake, there is always more love. Love engenders love. I later connected this with the Paschal candle, a symbol of Christ. The flame is distributed and is never exhausted.

To me Iris was a very good friend who has been with me most of my life.

Iris Murdoch – My Godmother

Ben MacIntyre

On my desk, as I write, is an antique red leather card-carrying case, now somewhat battered from years of travel. It was given to me by Iris when I was about ten years old, after a marathon poker session on a rainy day in the Scottish Highlands.

That summer, having just seen 'The Sting' starring Paul Newman and Robert Redford, I had decided to become a professional gambler. We discussed this new career plan all afternoon, as I contrived to lose a small fortune in matchsticks. Two weeks later the card case arrived, with a note explaining that it had belonged to Iris' mother and expressing the hope that it might be of use to me when I got to Chicago.

I do not think Iris was remotely interested in cards, and was doubtless aware that the passion of a child's wet afternoon would change as fast as the weather, but the card case was somehow confirmation of her interest in me, By the time the present arrived, I suspect I had already forgotten my gambling ambitions but Iris, characteristically, had not.

It was my supreme good fortune to have a Godmother not only extraordinarily generous with her own enthusiasm, but equally determined to kindle and feed my own, however fleeting: after cards it was fishing, then P.G. Wodehouse, then cricket, briefly God, then girls, then history, then publishing, then journalism, then writing. Iris treated each of these, my childish and then adult obsessions, with the same gravity and intensity. Iris has always made me feel like the central character in a most important novel. Whatever my latest preoccupation, I knew she would follow the plot, add a new twist, keep reading into the next chapter, with a talent to inspire that millions have also found in her writing.

My late father, Angus Macintyre, who should have been writing this tribute, was similarly sustained by Iris' intellect and friendship throughout his adult life. When he was elected President of Hertford College, many sent congratulatory notes, but Iris wrote a three-page essay explaining exactly why this was an inspired appointment. Like every good literary Godmother, Iris gave book-tokens, but she also gave lasting tokens of her confidence and enthusiasm. My father always kept her letter near at hand, as I have kept my red card case.

Iris Bayley:
A tribute in small change

Eric Christiansen

Iris became a friend about thirty-three years ago, when I was a younger colleague of John Bayley. This is not a long stretch, compared to the duration of most of her friendships; but it seems to deserve some sort of thanksgiving, even in the form of trivial reminiscence.

In those days, her amiability was puzzling. Was it kindness? Pity for the intellectually infirm? Or was it a sort of transferred pastoral concern, something the wives of older fellows did, to prevent the young ones going sour too soon? At any rate, it was a blessing: a life-line from a brighter world to the half-lit routine of history tutoring. But it was possible to draw a wage from an English university and still care so little for the things that mainly concerned Iris; her strongest appeal was her capacity for cheering people up. She had a kind face, seldom betraying impatience at the opinions of others, and was game for almost any sort of social experience short of stag-hunting. New College Quad has many admirable properties, but gaiety was not one of them; except when Iris used to drop in for a picnic.

At first, there were misunderstandings about the ingredients. Indoor picnics of that era tended to include a few small eggs, some ersatz caviar, runny cheese, and a chicory salad dressed with nine parts of oil and one of lemon-juice. The aim was not to satisfy hunger but to do the right thing by the guest. In this respect, it misfired. She never actually flung her plate to the floor, or threw the eggs out of the window; but she brought the feeding business down to earth. She would arrive with a shopping basket from which she supplied the neglected essentials. Bread, always white. English cheese, by the pound, not the triangle: waxy and unimpressionable. Butter: slabs, not pats, in white paper, from New Zealand. Ham with plenty of fat and bread-crumbs about it. No pansy pastries from Palm's: the true jam-tart, as served to the boys of the Remove. So there was food on the table;

the food she brought; and a small stock behind the door, in case something went wrong. After a while, I got it right.

Less easily, the intellectual part of the picnic. As a novel-reader, I assumed that her main business was writing them, and that philosophy was a task from which the profits of fiction had freed her. It was hard to imagine that anyone possessed of the most enviable of talents, that of making the improbable seem real, should waste her time doing the opposite. But talk about fiction revealed a lack of common ground. Here is a peevish note from the early seventies:

> *Iris not a great reader of novels. She is a reader of great novels. Her view of literature is along an airy corridor, decorated with statues: Plato, Dante, Shakespeare, Dickens & Co.*

She certainly didn't view it as a cross-section of the London underground during rush-hour. She happily denied any knowledge of many less-than-Shakespearian works, and when asked whether her selection of the significant few masterpieces were not capricious, or even accidental, she answered:

> *No, it is not. Their ideas are the valuable ones. None of us could face life without them, so to speak. And at least we know that they had them. Look here, if you can find some other chaps who had them first, you must let me know their names.*

This cut out some empty words about unmemorable works. She wanted at least a hint of greatness in what she read, and she knew where to find it. It was Bryan Magee who got her to define art as 'close dangerous play with unconscious forces', but unfortunately not in time to save me from telling her the merits of authors who worked on different principles, such as Surtees or Lord Berners.

Nevertheless, for the purposes of her own novels she liked getting the small things right, and she collected details. When told that A had thrown her drink at B and had then bitten C in the leg, she asked:

> *Now (to rhyme with 'flow', rather than 'bough') at what point exactly did she say those words? 'I have been wanting to do this for a very long time'? After the wine was thrown. Or it wouldn't have been a surprize,*

and she might have missed. Would she not have said 'do that', rather than 'this', if the action were completed?

Possibly. But it was after. I know it wasn't during.

Look here, this is not by any chance fiction, is it?

Then there was the trouble with history: one of her favourite subjects, despite its essential lack of satisfactory conclusions and its record of unalleviated pain. Her questions were usually about the things that historians are not expected to discuss; certainly not qualified, anyway. She wanted some kind of moral autopsy. She wanted a meaning. So, to check these disturbing tendencies, I answered her questions with a flow of directionless anecdote, sagas of futile endeavour and moral equivocation. In vain. She listened patiently to the Schleswig-Holstein Question, more than once; to the story of the great Paraguayan war; to the colonisation of Greenland, and to the decline of the Icelandic commonwealth; to almost anything that might escape incorporation into a larger picture. In vain. Having listened, she would ask with a smile:

But these chaps. I suppose they were, in their way, aware, so to speak, of a greater good?

'All too aware' was not the right answer. It was better to keep off Ireland, since even Iris finds the end-results of that history discouraging. Poland was a different matter. 'Ah, the Poles,' she would say; and her face lit up, as if, in that case, the tribulations of the past had been endured to some purpose, and the devil had been defeated not so much in battle as in argument. Not that she had an irrational aversion to armed conflict. When I mentioned a friend whose great regret was that he had not been born in time to play a part in the Second World War, she agreed that that indeed was a time when all good men had felt obliged to enlist.

Absolutely. And yet I find it easy to imagine that having found himself in the front line for the best of motives, a good man might still throw down his rifle and run.

Well, he wouldn't get very far.

Why not ?

Because I find it easy to imagine that I would be his officer, standing with a revolver directly behind him.

Once, she came right out with it, and. assured me that there was no understanding history without understanding Hegel. I muttered that his Philosophy of History appeared to be utter drivel. She replied, with the impatience of a saint:

Of course, it's no good attempting that unless you begin with the Phenomenology of Mind.

That was not a corker; it was a good laugh. There were many more, on less solemn pretexts.

Gossip should have played a large part in these meetings, but it didn't, because she is not very good at it. Her intense interest in others is untainted by malice, or by adverse comment of any kind directed towards any individual. With groups, it is different; now and then she let fly at a number of barn-doors, such as progressive education, but not so virulently as to puncture any named progressive educator. This kindness was no doubt insufferable for the true gossip of the Bowra school, but I never hear her friends complain at her preference for discussing heroes rather than villains.

On the days when friends were gathered near the snappish log fires in the micro-baronial back room of Cedar Lodge, Steeple Aston, there were no dull moments. She and John were all the better hosts for seeming to be guests at their own parties, while not losing interest in those who were there by invitation. She had a way of staring down at her glass, as if she were listening very carefully to the speaker. As indeed she may have been, but she was also indicating that the glass was empty. She loved the crowded room, the voices, the possibility of multiplying pleasure through many conversations; and that, with the help of John, is not the least of her achievements, however evanescent it seems in comparison with the rest.

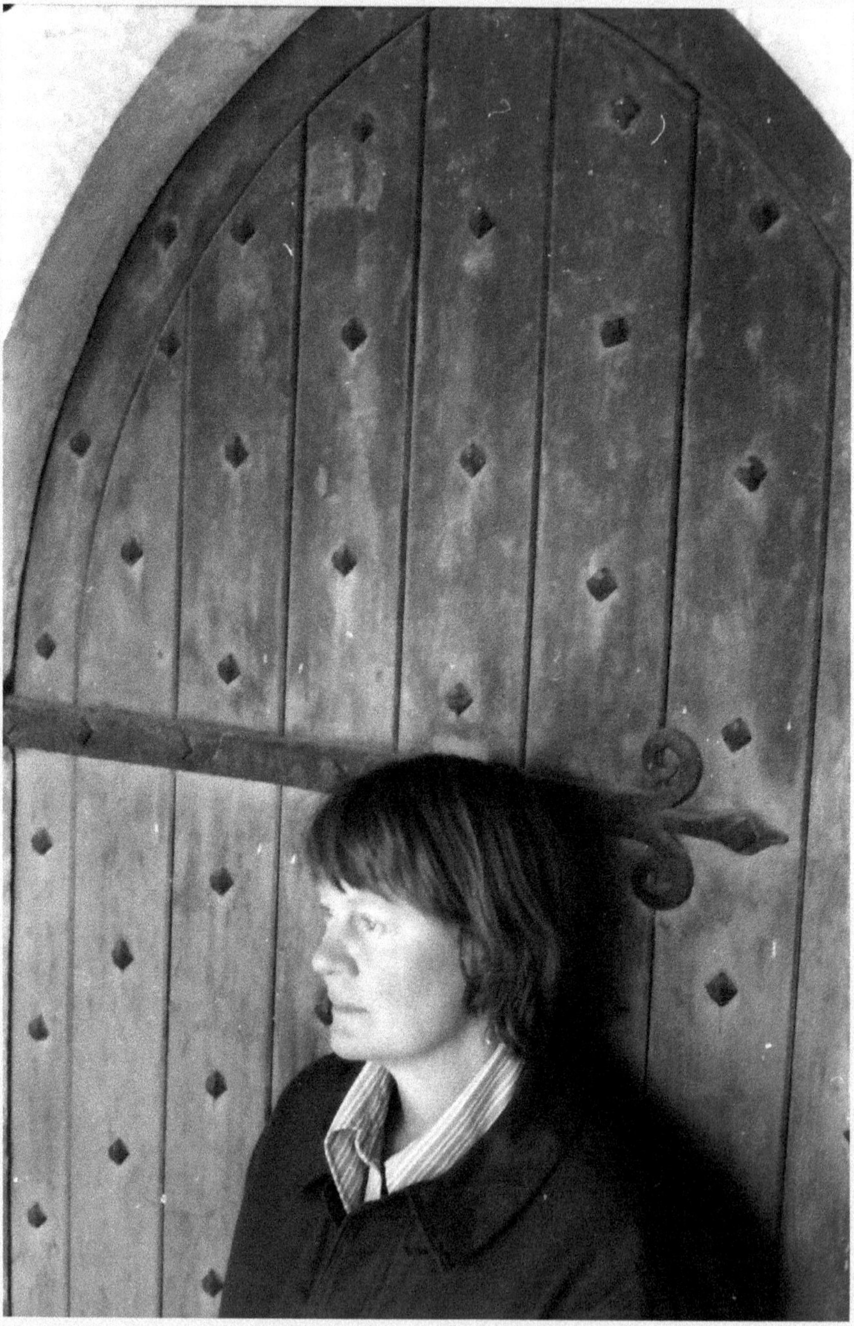

Travels with the Bayleys

John Grigg

John Bayley and I were friends from school days, and we married at much the same time (he in 1956, I two years later). From the moment he introduced me to Iris I was sure that she, too, would become a very dear friend, and so it has proved. Though perhaps rather intimidated by the idea of her, I felt at once, on meeting her, that she was a person of rare warmth and sweetness. In turn my own wife, Patsy, formed an instant attachment to both the Bayleys, and they evidently to her. Over the years we have spent quite a lot of time together, not least travelling abroad (a test that only solid friendships can survive).

In the summer of 1963 we went to Russia, approaching it slowly by way of Denmark, Sweden and Finland. The last lap of our journey consisted of a whole day spent in a Russian train from Helsinki to Leningrad. The train crawled along, as though reluctant to leave Finland's precariously free air. The seats in our compartment were very hard, and between them there was a table with a faded pot-plant and an electric lamp that did not work. On this table an aged attendant placed, every hour, tall glasses of tea set in holders of figured tin or pewter. The tea was brewed in a samovar at the end of our carriage, over a stick fire, and when the train stopped between stations, as it often did, the old man would climb down to replenish his supply of sticks. By contrast with this primitive scene the Russians were at the same time rocketing a woman into Space – all normal economic development being sacrificed to their Cold War rivalry with the Americans.

There was no restaurant car on the train, and only a few tasteless biscuits accompanied the regular supply of tea, so we (the Griggs) were grateful for a share of the salami that the Bayleys had prudently bought in Helsinki. Sugar lumps for the tea came in paper wrapping with a Russian word on it that stumped even John. Iris said 'I suppose it's the name of the chap who made it', and had to be reminded that in the Soviet Union chaps did not make things, in that sense. (We later discovered that it was the word for 'refined').

Eventually Leningrad unfolded itself in the white night as we circled the city to the October Station, where we were met and driven to our hotel, the Europe. There we had to fill in forms giving a mass of information about ourselves, including our date of arrival and – a sinister touch – our gate of 'supposed' departure. We soon realised that we were at a great disadvantage in being individual tourists rather than members of a group. To the Soviet bureaucracy individuals were automatically suspect, as well as less easy to manage. Even groups were kept waiting a longish time for meals, but we had to wait much longer – anything up to two hours, with only the solace of a carafe of vodka while we waited. The first night we had a bottle of Georgian wine as well, with some caviare, after which we were ready for bed.

The hotel was magnificent in scale, but seedy and decrepit. (I wonder what it is like now). We could not, however, complain of the size of our bedrooms. Ours was large enough for a dance and had the right sort of floor (parquet). But the effect of the room and its imposing furniture was let down by a huge ashtray full of cigarette-ends and an unemptied wastepaper basket. In the dingy bathroom the basin had no plug, but the bath had one, and above all there was hot water. The Bayleys' accommodation (on a different floor) was suitably grander than ours: a sitting room as well as a bedroom and an even larger writing table. But the downside was that their supply of hot water was intermittent and there was no W in the WC. They did not mention this to the management (possibly assuming it would be a waste of time to do so), but one morning when John was sitting on the loo the bathroom was suddenly invaded by a female housekeeper leading a gang of burly men, who set to work on the pipes oblivious of his presence.

During our stay we had a tourist guide called Nina, who showed us the sights and no doubt reported on our conversation. Unusually for a Russian she had little humour, and was altogether rather a tough little nut. Her English, learnt without benefit of any contact with the outside world, was near-perfect, but she did commit one idiomatic lapse which we did not bother to correct. Pointing to one of the innumerable posters of Khrushchev (Soviet dictator at the time) she described him as 'our so-called prime minister'. Nina took us to all the splendid palaces bequeathed by the Tsars, and restored at vast cost by the current regime, but she appeared to be totally ignorant of Russian history before 1917. At our request, and with obvious reluctance, she also took us to one of the few Orthodox churches in the city that were 'operational' (her word), and to a small Roman Catholic church whose white-washed simplicity suggested a Nonconformist conventicle. The priest, an Estonian, received us with touching delight and stood waving outside the church as we drove away. His must have been a lonely life. Iris and Patsy were in tears as we left him, and probably John and I were too.

In January 1967 we were with the Bayleys in India. A general election was in progress, in which Iris' schoolfriend from Badminton, Indira Gandhi, was seeking a new mandate as prime minister. While we were in Bombay the Bayleys made a foray to Aurangabad, where Mrs Gandhi met them by chance at the airport and, immediately recognising Iris, came across and talked to her for some time, despite the pressure of the campaign. Later, in Delhi, we had dinner with her. On that occasion she told us she had become prime minister partly because the Indian people regarded her as more religious than her father, Jawaharlal Nehru. Were they right, we asked? No, she replied with an almost cynical smile, in some ways she was even less so. He was more romantic and emotional than she was. Besides, women in general were more down-to-earth than men.

At another dinner in Delhi our host, the wise and charming M.C. Chagla (then external affairs minister), who had recently read *The Red and the Green*, suggested to Iris that she write a novel about India. She did not dismiss the idea out of hand, and said that she had had 'an illumination' in the Elephanta Caves. But whatever it may have been her passage to India did not, sadly, inspire a novel. Old pupils of hers seemed thick on the ground in India, and admirers were, of course, legion. But at one party in Bombay she was greeted in a different capacity, to her own amusement and relief, when a glamorous Indian woman, having ascertained that she was Iris Murdoch, said 'Oh then I know your mother-in-law'. The lady and Mrs Bayley senior had, it transpired, been neighbours some years before in a Kent village, and fellow members of the local Women's Institute. Iris was keen to see Varanesi (Benares), so the Bayleys went there for a day or two after Delhi, while we went straight to Madras. When they re-joined us there it was clear that Varanesi had appealed more to Iris than to John;

he described it as 'a mixture of Lourdes and Southend.' For their Indian journey the Bayleys had equipped themselves with a generous supply of gin, carried in a plastic bottle which had formerly contained Stergene. Much as we appreciated it in places where liquor was hard to come by, some mental effort was needed, when drinking from it, to banish all thought of the bottle's original use.

Later, we went on a Swan Hellenic cruise with the Bayleys – a fortnight of enchantment among the Greek islands. Since I was writing about it for a newspaper with expenses paid the accommodation advantage was reversed compared with Leningrad; the Bayleys, paying for themselves had a miserable cabin apparently below the waterline, whereas ours was relatively comfortable. I say 'relatively', because physical luxury was not the salient feature of the old cruise ship S.S. Orpheus (formerly the Irish packet S.S .Munster). The ship had a distinct list, which meant that having a shower always carried the risk of flooding our cabin. But a dodgy shower was better than no shower at all, and the cabin was fairly spacious. It became, therefore, the normal meeting-place for the four of us when we were not engaged in cultural activities ashore.

Our fellow-passengers, who were more like fellow-pilgrims, seemed to include many people to whom the cruise was the fulfilment of a lifetime's dream. The jet set was totally absent. Our British lecturers on the ship were all star performers, and the Greek guides (mainly women), who took over from them on land, did us equally proud. The Bayleys were in their element in such company. Iris, with her background of classical scholarship, and her imagination – so like that of the ancient Greeks – in which an intense awareness of ordinary life is shot through with magic and myth, was in a sense coming home.

Two occasions stand out in my memory of the trip. On Delos we played truant from the sight-seeing to bathe in a little cove on the south side of the island. At a moment when only my wife was still in the sea a single large wave came from nowhere and almost dashed her against the rocks. There was not a breath of wind, and no sign of any vessel between us and the horizon. Besides, why just one wave? What mysterious power could have caused it? The incident seemed to come straight from one of Iris' novels. The other somewhat surreal occasion was a Sunday communion service conducted by one of our lecturers, Owen Chadwick, as Orpheus was passing through the Corinth canal. Iris and John both attended it, responding clearly to the many associations that it stirred. Without subscribing to any doctrine, both are, in their different ways, more truly religious than many formal believers; John in the easy-going Anglican tradition, Iris in the visionary tradition of early Irish and Scottish Christianity.

On our travels together I have been struck by Iris' persistent letter-writing, and when I once asked her about this she said that she was replying to people who had written to her about her books. Considering how many fans she must have throughout the world, I am awestruck at the thought of her writing to so many of them – perhaps all of them – in her own hand. Murdochian is a widely accepted and understood word; because she belongs to the select group of writers, in any age, whose view of the world has required the invention of an adjective.

Thirty-Five Years of Memories of Iris Murdoch

Miklos Veto (trans. Justin Broackes)

On the ground of my participation in the anti-soviet Revolution of 1956, I was due to be condemned to a heavy prison sentence. I regarded myself therefore as having no option but to flee the Hungary in which I had been born and raised. After three months in a refugee camp in Yugoslavia, I managed to reach France. I ended up completing a licence in Philosophy at the Sorbonne in 1959. But what was to be my future? The question presented itself in an acute form. I wanted to be an academic, but to be able to get a position in public service, you had to be French. To be naturalized, you had to live in France for five years. To live, however, you had to earn your living. And, to earn your living, you had to have a position! There was no option but to leave France. To leave France for the USA where, at that time, it was still relatively easy to get university work. One difficulty remained. In the United States, people teach in English. Now, besides my native Hungarian, I had done some French, German and Russian, but no English. In order to learn English, I managed to get a little scholarship for 10 months in England. When Jean Wahl, one of my masters at the Sorbonne, heard that I was going to leave for Oxford, he gave me a letter of recommendation addressed to a certain Isaiah Berlin, of whose name even I was at that time quite unaware. Sir Isaiah welcomed me in All Souls College in an immense study whose walls were covered with portraits of bewigged clergymen from the 17th and 18th centuries. He was pleasant but very short of time. Yes, what you are interested in is the philosophy and sociology of religion. Yes, I will arrange for you to be awarded a four-year scholarship for a D.Phil. and I will send you to see the Warden of St Antony's College. I was dumbstruck but I neither could nor wished to say no.

I was first directed to a brilliant young American sociologist, Norman Birnbaum. Mr Birnbaum was Mr, not Dr, because at that time only the doctorates of Cambridge and Trinity College Dublin were recognized as equivalent to the Oxford D. Phil., and he possessed only a Ph.D. from Harvard. I got on well with Birnbaum, but we realized quickly that if religion was for me an essential theme, it was by way of philosophy that I was going to find it again. I ended up choosing as the subject of my thesis the work of Simone Weil. I had learned that the mother of Simone Weil was still alive. I accordingly wrote to her to request a meeting. I was living at St Antony's College and one day, coming down to go and eat lunch, I found in my 'pigeon hole' a letter from Paris. The sender of it was: S. W. I was a little shocked, for if I believe in the Catholic teaching on the other world, I did not imagine there was a postal service that reached it. The letter was in fact from the pen of Madame Selma Weil, the mother of Simone. Shortly afterwards, I was sent to see Iris Murdoch – one of the rare Oxford teachers of philosophy who knew and loved the author of *Attente de Dieu* (*Waiting on God*) – on the subject of my work.

Iris was 41 years old when she agreed to supervise my thesis. If Isaiah Berlin and the people at my college had turned to her, the reason is that it was the age of Oxford Philosophy, at its most active and most virulent, and neither Simone Weil nor I had anything to do with this school. People of great stature like Gilbert Ryle and A. J. Ayer held the most important chairs of Philosophy, a man like P. F. Strawson was beginning to be known. It was clear that none of these people could be considered as a director of my research. Isaiah Berlin initially thought that we should ask Charles Taylor to agree to be my supervisor. This young Canadian philosopher was brilliant, profound, and into the bargain, he was a Catholic like me. But hardly had Berlin uttered his name, when he realized it was impossible. Taylor was certainly of high intellectual standing and he was four years my senior, but he was not yet a Doctor. Iris, evidently, wasn't either – and wasn't going to become one either, other than a Doctor honoris causa – but for her generation of British academics, the doctorate was a non-entity. If you had got a First in your BA, you could become a 'don' or 'tutor' of a College. If in later years you wrote something important, you might be appointed Professor. So we turned to Iris Murdoch. Iris had been at St Anne's College for more than ten years. She knew Oxford Philosophy very well, her first writings had been composed in the setting of that world, but she was more and more severe in her judgement of it. She was very close to the French thought of the time, especially Sartre – to whom she had devoted her first book – and Gabriel Marcel. As she wrote in one of her very first texts: 'It is not clear… on what ground the hygienic and dehydrated analysis of mental concepts which we use in this city [Oxford]

can claim to be more accurate than the more lush efforts of M. Marcel'.
Now, besides these 'negative' qualifications for being 'supervisor' of a
student who belonged to a non-Oxford philosophical world, there was
another reason, a positive one, which pushed Iris Murdoch to accept the
task. Iris, who had read Simone Weil as far back as 1947 in Cambridge,
was passionate about this marvellous philosophical writer, who had died at
the age of 34, some 150 kms from Oxford. The author of *The Bell* felt close
to Simone Weil, who she would consider as one of the most important
thinkers of our time. And she must have thought she would be able to
work better on her if she took on a student preparing a thesis on this
philosopher, who had been born hardly ten years before her, but who was
already known and read in every country in the West.

I went to see Iris for the first time in October 1960. Living at St Antony's, I
had only to cross the little road which separated the college from her own,
St Anne's. She welcomed me kindly, she listened to me with sympathy and
then went on to say: Could you give me a bibliography on Simone Weil?
Thereafter, every week or every two weeks, dressed in my black gown,
I went to see her. We would talk about Simone Weil, about philosophy,
about my past. She let me talk, from time to time she asked me questions,
but she never talked about herself. I knew that she was married, that she
didn't live in Oxford itself, and that she wrote novels. She knew by this
time that I was engaged, and suddenly she said to me, 'Tell me about
your fiancée'! I didn't need to be asked twice and went on to pour forth
a dithyramb about Odile. Shortly afterwards, when Odile made her first
visit to Oxford, we were entertained in Iris' study. She had invited for the
occasion Enid Starkie, the very well-known historian of literature. Miss
Starkie had no objection to whisky, of which there was a large bottle on
Iris' table. As for the young girl from a good family who was my fiancée,
she was a little surprised and, even more, embarrassed.

We were getting married the following year and Iris gave us a most useful
present: a magnificent little Finnish red casserole. It will travel with us to
America and will die, after several decades of good and useful service, a
natural death. We will spend the first year of our marriage in Oxford, in a
little flat situated behind St Antony's where Iris will come to visit. We had
nothing to offer but a glass of good West Country cider, which Iris loved,
like the characters in *The Bell*. But she was not content with giving us a
kitchen utensil and drinking our cider. She gave us 'practical' help. Odile
was just finishing her thesis on Dante and Claudel at the Sorbonne, but she

did not have a scholarship for Oxford. My scholarship was just sufficient for the two of us and Iris made several interventions to help Odile to find work. She ended up getting some French tutorials, paid at a suitable rate, at St Claire's Hall, the most chic of the 'finishing schools' of Oxford. So two or three young girls from (very) good families would arrive at our place once a week, dressed, too, in a black gown. A little bit of oral history: Odile was improving her English at a good language school in the city. She did translations there from French into English. Now, the English girls in her tutorials needed to do proses from English into French. Odile therefore gave them some of her translations – duly corrected by her English teacher – which these elegant young girls would go on to translate back into French.

Our first year of marriage was 1962-63. Odile defended her thesis in Paris in June 1963, and I was to defend mine some weeks later. Iris had a very high opinion of my work. She who often would correct my English ended up writing to me that from now on, I had style. And she even recommended the publication of my thick manuscript to the renowned publisher Victor Gollancz who asked her if she would write an introduction. I was very glad to have written my text, I was aware of having done a unique piece of work and I presented myself, very sure of myself, to my two examiners. They were two good Oxford philosophers, but with sympathies for 'continental' philosophy. Things unfortunately went very badly. I was – it seems – rather arrogant: I even asked one of my examiners if he didn't regret not being God. … The response was a furious No. The interrogation lasted for seven hours and I ended up being 'referred', or effectively failed, which is very rare for theses at Oxford. Iris will find this very distressing; she will write a long letter of protest to Gilbert Ryle who was at this time in charge of Philosophy at Oxford University. But there was nothing to be done; I would have to go through the examination again. I would try to make some changes and corrections to the text, but the whole process would not amount to much. As for Iris, she would write to me that the problem was not rewriting the thesis, but finding other examiners (18 December 1963). The examiners, however, remained the same. But they evidently changed their opinion, and in June 1964, a year therefore after my botched defence, I ended up being declared D. Phil. Oxon. The good news reached me in Milwaukee just as we were finishing our first year of teaching at Marquette University.

After just under three years of meetings in person and oral exchanges, it will be written correspondence. Iris remains interested in what is becoming of me personally and philosophically, but the ties slowly become less tight. Separation in space and time explains this distancing between people. And yet Iris – I don't know if she was like this in her behaviour with all of her old thesis students – remains loyal and replies every time. Rereading her letters, I wonder if I shouldn't have been more loyal myself. I will write to her mainly about things involving my interests and then the interests of our children. The correspondence is relatively intense in the first year in America. Iris wants to help me get over my setback. She is relieved when I end up getting my D. Phil. from Oxford. She will congratulate me on my appointment at Yale (Autumn 1964). But she had also announced how happy she was at the fresh air she was breathing, after having given up teaching in Oxford, when lecturing in London (15 June 1964). The second part of these memories relates therefore to a period when we will no longer have anything but epistolary contact. Iris would very kindly constantly ask when we would see each other again, but years went by without a meeting being possible. In the end, after the World Congress of Philosophy in Brighton in 1988, I spent two days in Oxford and the second day I went, without announcing myself, to her house. I rang the bell at 68 Hamilton Road. John Bayley, interrupting his breakfast, came to open the door for me. I had a quick conversation with Iris and … we said nothing very much.

These epistolary contacts lasted 32 years but it was mainly the first eight which were interesting. The beginning had quite a lot of excitement to it. Iris was furious at the judgement of my examiners. She viewed it as an 'injustice' (June 1964). And, above all: she had just left the University of Oxford, and lo and behold, her last thesis student had been failed. What is more, the fact that it involved a thesis on Simone Weil, an author wholly ignored by Oxford Philosophy, must have added to her bitter disappointment. In the final analysis, she felt she had been humiliated. If you had been permanently failed, she wrote to me, 'I would have been left (myself) with a sense of (my) failure'. She will recover from her emotions once I have my title of Doctor. From that moment on, her letters will contain several remarks that are interesting even for the evolution of her thought. During my third year at Yale, I had some difficulties with the department of Philosophy where I was teaching and was wondering if I should get myself appointed elsewhere, perhaps in a department of Religion or Theology. She wrote to me at that time: 'I have always felt that you were properly a theologian. (I recall your saying to me some years ago that your philosophy always turned into theology: so does mine: which is awkward for me as I don't believe in God)' (December 1967). But we also had some more significant exchanges on the subject of the evolution of her own philosophical work. We know that Iris had already read something of or on Heidegger as early as the 1950s. I myself was beginning to study the German thinker closely in 1965. I wrote to Iris about this and she thanked me for my 'splendid Heidegger letter … (I have put it inside my copy of *Sein und Zeit* as a charm)' (early 1965). Then, in another letter a little later: 'Oddly enough I am trying to … read Heidegger just now. I tried in German but gave up, alas… I struggled with him earlier but could never make up my mind'. And she reacts to my critical comments. Yes, he 'is uncanny, dangerous'. Somewhat later, she will write to me about the great work by the philosopher of Freiburg: 'I have only so far read one third of the book … It is certainly by a remarkable philosopher. I feel so far though … that part of the job has been done better by Wittgenstein (I think it is largely the same job though)' (Spring 1965). Then she apologizes for not having written for some time: 'I put off writing because I wanted to collect my wits about Heidegger but now other things have come between me and *Sein und Zeit* and I am not likely to have any sensible opinions about that work for some time (if ever).' No doubt towards the end of the 1980s, Iris will begin writing on the thought of Heidegger, but she will not manage to complete her work. On the other hand, she tells that she is working on Plato, Plato in whom 'the whole truth' is to be found. And she adds the sentence: 'You may imagine, dear boy, from whom I derived this intuition' (6 May 1965). She means of course Simone Weil. A Simone Weil who has never ceased to be a source or inspiration for this great novelist and for this excellent philosopher. Shortly after our arrival in Milwaukee, I read *The Unicorn* and I ask Iris if her novel is not inspired by the writer of the *Notebooks*? 'No, you are not dreaming about *The Unicorn*,' she replies, 'it is full of Simone Weil though few are those who spot that greater source of my wisdom' (October-November 1963). Another eight years and I will be able to send her my thesis rewritten as a book. She is delighted to see the work in print. And she remarks with her habitual modesty, 'It reminds me of so many things you taught me'.

Between 1971 and 1985, there is a break in our correspondence. She resumes only at the time when our eldest, Etienne Emanuel, a normalien, is due to spend a semester visiting a British university and I ask for some help from Iris, who will try to do what she can. In fact, she had known of the existence of Etienne practically from the time of his birth. We had sent her some photos of the baby, and she acknowledged with delight these 'splendid photos'. 'I am,' she wrote, 'delighted. What a look of formidable intelligence and thereness on the face of that very small creature… I wish I could be a godmother to E. E. but (even if I were asked) it could be technically impossible for at least two reasons … but perhaps I might elect myself to be a sort of honorary one' (early 1965). Twenty-eight years later, when she hears of our son's decision to commit himself on the path that will lead him to the Catholic priesthood, she rushes to declare, 'I hope he will be Pope' (12 January 1993). Her last letter is dated 30 January 1995. She congratulates us on the marriage photos of our daughter Marie-Elisabeth – normalienne and doctor, too, as well as the mother of four children – who she finds 'so beautiful'. And she concludes her letter: 'I am writing another novel but very slowly'. This novel will never be completed. Iris is embarking on the path of Alzheimer's disease, which will plunge her into the loss of all memory and will lead her to death.

Translator's note.
I have aimed, in consultation with the author, to retain the careful usage of tenses in the original, which is distinctive of the original French. The result is an idiom that sounds perhaps slightly more unusual in English than in French; the result conveys, I hope, something quite characteristic in the precision of the original.

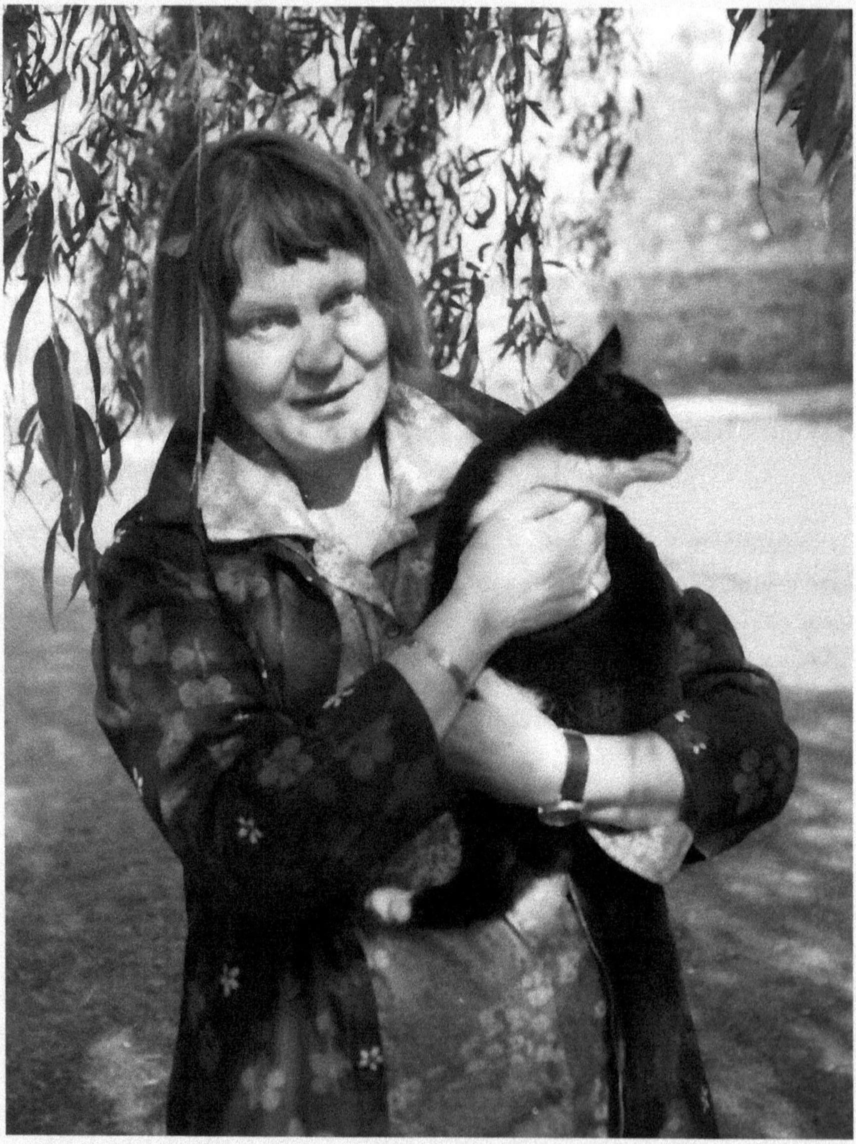

Editing Iris Murdoch

Carmen Callil

I first met Iris in 1983 when I took over as Publisher at Chatto and Windus (having founded Virago Press) from Norah Smallwood, Iris' friend and publisher for many years. It was a hard thing to move from someone like Norah Smallwood, to a younger woman, who came with a reputation as a wayward feminist publisher. How was Iris to know that politically correct feminism was my bête noire? After a few soundings on this front, at our very first lunch, the matter was dismissed forever, and we laid down a pattern that was to continue until I left Chatto ten years later.

This is how it was to be Iris' publisher. Every now and then a phone call would come: 'Carmen dear, I've finished a novel'. Iris would then arrive carrying the handwritten manuscript in those blue plastic holdalls so useful for taking clothes to the laundrette. Thousands of pages carefully punctuated and paragraphed exactly as Iris wanted, handwriting only just decipherable. I remember, painfully, when one of my editors changed her punctuation: this was the only time I ever saw a flush of anger on Iris' cheeks. This bag of paper laundry turned without any troubles into *The Book and The Brotherhood*, *The Philosopher's Pupil*, *The Good Apprentice* and many more.

Iris was a joy to publish: kind and good and understanding. But always the best thing about her is what goes on in her mind: and the time allotted for this was the splendid lunches we had once or twice a year, sometimes with John, sometimes not. Though we were born on the same day, in every other way Iris and I are totally unalike. This was most evident during these lunches. Though we consumed the same amount of food and drink – Iris is a good trencherwoman – food disappears down my throat in a vulgar rush. Iris eats so slowly that sometimes we'd be sitting in the restaurant well after 3 with Iris still toying with her first lettuce leaf. But the conversation! Wonderful.

Those were the Thatcher years, and Iris was an admirer – I was not – but we never argued: Thatcher was a philosopher's stone which gave Iris the opportunity to pounce on the subjects and ideas of the day with her gimlet brain, her kind heart, and her brilliant mind. But we covered a thousand other things: mothers (always a favourite subject), Ireland, books... Leaving her to return to the office was a wrench, and a thudding return to the everyday. There was something Homeric about knowing and working for Iris, because above all she is a master storyteller. Added to that she is a spellbinder – on the page and in herself too: there's a bit of the devil in Iris – an Irish Leprechaun kind of spirit doing only good in the world.

Iris and Brigid: A Sketch

Kate Levey

Assuming exaggerated Irish tones, my mother would begin, 'Look here...' or 'I say, old thing...' and instantly my father and I knew our supper table would be enlivened by some anecdote featuring Iris. In private Brigid had a good line in sardonic wit. Although her mimicry was, I think, imperfect, she caught Iris' breathy manner of speech; anyway we readily laughed at the pseudo-Iris she presented to us.

My mother's irreverence, far from being savage, was an affirmation of relaxed acceptance and affection. Iris and Brigid had long been intimate; after some years their turbulent love affair had dissolved, leaving a firm friendship upon which both were resolved. From the very start Iris Murdoch and Brigid Brophy disagreed about almost everything, yet the bond between the two writers survived in one form or other until broken after forty years by Brigid's death.

My father Michael Levey was present when Iris and Brigid first met, in 1954. He was struck by their immediate rapport. Not long after, when Iris visited their London flat, Michael records the pair arguing uninhibitedly about Greek philosophers: Iris was for Plato's pre-eminence while Brigid argued for Aristotle's. My father remarks that to this he could 'bring nothing but attention to refilling the two participants' glasses'.

Iris became part of my parents' lives. She was never a rival of Michael's for Brigid's love.

Sometimes the Bayleys joined my parents for the opera or dinner, but usually, I believe, Iris visited my mother at home, my youth perhaps making that the most pragmatic arrangement. Michael knew about Iris and Brigid's relationship; Brigid kept nothing from him. Individually my parents were fond of Iris: each admired her unconventional style, and acknowledged her charm; they both enjoyed her wit, but they also shared a metaphorical raised eyebrow at her idiosyncrasy, her occasional naivete. She crops up (sometimes starkly as 'Murdoch') in their letters, such as in this from Brigid to Michael in Italy, which bears the footnote: 'Letter from Iris inviting herself to luncheon next Thursday – I don't mean we need eat anything – I'll bring some wine and we can while away the afternoon...'

Thankfully my mother did not forget she had me, then a baby or toddler, at home that afternoon, though it scuppered Iris' plan. As a child I found Iris a woollen, or tweedy, figure who was shyly awkward face to face; rather than interest, she evinced a benign bemusement at my existence. It is recognised, I think, that she didn't have a parental bone in her body, yet Iris was a most generous giver of gifts to me, by way of which, additionally, she honoured my mother.

Disagreement between Iris and Brigid never abated. From politics to Christmas traditions, they did not see eye to eye. It is my view that the chief divergence they suffered – and both did emotionally suffer – had its nub in the matter of candour. To Brigid the clear, quotidian truth, as opposed to muddle, evasions or deceptions, held a price above rubies because it signalled ultimate, exclusive love. For Iris, this was in Brigid a troubling, troublesome foible.

My father recounts how during one visit Iris 'suddenly got to her feet' and announced that she must go; she 'departed in mystery', he writes, commenting,

> Before we understood her need for secrecy, and even occasionally afterwards, as a tease, we would casually enquire about her destination. All one was told, with patent reluctance, was that she was awaited in some unspecified location by 'a person'.

Finding no accommodation possible between them, Iris and my mother were damaged irreparably and in 1967 Brigid finally broke away. Whether Iris clung on insistently at this point, I don't know. John Bayley said in 1999 (*In the Psychiatrist's Chair*, BBC Radio 4) that Iris 'always fell in love with top class people' and this leads me to suspect Iris may have rather desperately wanted to remain Brigid's confidante, recognising my mother's mind as top class. They stayed in touch cordially, but much less intensely.

When, years later, Brigid was struck by multiple sclerosis, Iris was among the very few visitors she welcomed at Old Brompton Road; Iris Murdoch's loyalty was unshakeable. Later still, Iris made the hugely inconvenient journey to Louth in Lincolnshire, where my mother was in a nursing home. To get there, unless she was helicoptered in, Iris would have faced hours of travel, and might even have found a dulled and withdrawn Brigid by that late stage of illness. I was at work that day so my father saw Iris alone; I don't think they met again. The nursing care staff, to whom my mother was Lady Levey, might have enjoyed, had they but known of it, a visit from a Dame Commander of the British Empire, (not an everyday occurrence in Louth, I venture), but they probably saw instead, poignantly, two old women catching up, as time had caught up with them.

After my mother's death, Iris sent condolences to Michael, writing that Brigid was 'so beautiful, so brilliant, so loving, so witty, so brave'. Those words stand tribute equally and without qualification to Iris Murdoch herself.

Nuns and Soldiers: Iris in Provence

Lady Natasha Spender

We came to know Iris and John well in 1973 when, after some enjoyable times in Oxford and London, they accepted our summer invitation to 'Mas Saint Jerome', our cottage in Provence. Thereafter it became an annual visit over more than twenty years, memorable for its unique felicity.

As I stood waiting with an airport luggage *chariot* at the foot of the descending escalator for arrivals at Marseilles airport – and, I must own, suspecting that they might have missed the plane – there they finally appeared at the summit, gliding down in helpless laughter, though I no longer remember the joke. As the very last stragglers from the London flight they were surrounded by anxiously muttering Moroccans from Rabat, whilst their own fishing for innumerable bags and parcels had a sunnier air of somewhat distrait radiance. The tone we have always enjoyed with them from that first moment is one of gentle amusement. It is a constant – as if with one's normal body temperature goes a benign homeostatic level of spirit.

When all was stored in the car, it was fair to warn them that we would drive through the ugliest area in France, that of faceless furniture depots and giant oil refineries surrounding the Etang de Berre. But the Bayleys had not a care for these eyesores, and after skirting the wide flatlands of the Crau we drove into the most beautiful secret valley of the Alpille – that east-west chain of limestone mountains, small in size yet dramatic in scale which dominates the alluvial plain bordering the Mediterranean Sea. From Mouries the little dirt road wound through olive orchards and vineyards, past gushing canals and great patches of yellow scented broom amid the eccentric outcrops of limestone rock, eroded by wind and weather. Soon we were met in the driveway by Stephen in his frayed straw hat, smiling an affectionate welcome, and were immediately seated at table on the terrace, gazing at the 'frilly' (as Iris describes it) frieze of sun-whitened rocks touching the sky. (Her adjective recalls a local name for a similar limestone ridge a little further north, 'Les Dentelles de Montmirail'.) It was only after many annual visits that Iris felt so intimately in command of this landscape as to gather its many qualities into the powerful part it plays in *Nuns and Soldiers*.

A decade or so earlier when Stephen and I had first discovered this strangely beautiful land, we had felt possessed by its mystery and by the sense it gives one of antique gods – the upward surge of the limestone suggesting the overpowering gesture of some subterranean Pluto hurling them heavenwards. In this little outpost of the great Roman Empire 'in hither Gaul' one can scarcely help but feel an echo of the Roman sense of the implacable power of natural forces and the modest brevity of life for any human inhabitant. We are all fascinated by the changing aspect of the rocks throughout each day with the passage of the sun, from the etched clarity of sunrise to the midday brilliance and thence to the last coppery burnish before dusk and nightfall.

Within this diurnal rhythm our days fell into a pattern, my early morning gardening and weeding in the cool air often coinciding with the woodpecker sound of John's typewriter emanating from the furthest comer of the lilac walk. Occasionally Iris would silently join me, taking up without a word whichever tool was available and setting to with a calm pace and evident pleasure in the scents and sounds of early morning in the gradually warming opalescent light. Out of the companionable stretches of silence, our conversation arose in patches, sometimes with reflective pauses between question and answer. Were it not for the contented pace of our tasks and her gentle disposition, I could occasionally be reminded of those pauses more heavily laden with thought, of the seminars of Miss Anscombe in my student days. Yet Iris, who as she went to work with the secateurs might be answering my questions about Plato, or simply evoking with affection one of our mutual friends, would do so in a calm, almost Buddhist atmosphere of contemplation, sprinkled with gentle jokes or sudden concern for any living creature – 'I say, old thing, take care! There's a nice little nest of ants just by your left foot.' (In her presence, any gardener would feel shame for unthinking or murderous attitudes to wasps or the furry bumblebees she so adores.) One caught her compassionate attitude like an infection, however minute and unremarkable the creature; one could even come to love green-fly or red spiders. And when creatures were far from minuscule, the bright green and turquoise lizards or the huge grass snakes, the hoopoes and the owls, we both delighted in their friendly presence. The blend of clarity and benevolence in her discourse made of those early mornings a most refreshing interlude.

After a convivial breakfast on the terrace everyone disappeared to work, until in late morning Iris and John pottered off down the lane, very often for a dip in the agricultural canal. On our afternoon expeditions they were always ready to plunge in anywhere however rustic; strong-flowing rivers, the Durance or the Gardon, the wide beaches and huge Etangs or even the brackish puddles on the Camargue, as well as the scintillating pools of our neighbours. They could even coax me, an inveterate non-bather, into the shallow Etang d'Entresson. Iris wore a bathing tunic like those worn in my schooldays for Greek dancing, or when reciting in chorus the Gilbert Murray versions of Euripides. Her enthusiastic youthfulness in this garb gave me a sudden schoolgirl exuberance.

The part that water plays in her inner world is well-known, whether it be racing and turbulent or still. Water is either healing, or it is challenging as in *The Sea, The Sea* or in the Cumbrian episode of *Nuns and Soldiers* where it is life threatening. Amongst the rocks of the Alpilles there are a few natural pools, glassy and utterly still of surface, unless at ones approach there may be the plop of a frog seeking refuge. In sharp contrast is the ever-changing, winding strip of the *canal de Craponne*, made by that genius 16th century engineer who thus brought the fertility which transformed this arid land. There are stretches where its rapid flow is serene, or there is tumultuous, frothing spray as it tumbles down a chute, the sound overpowering our voices. In the novel Iris makes a kind of collage of several far-flung focal points of her daily wanderings, concentrating them into a small area whereby their role is apparently to force the main characters to face their true selves and the turmoil through which they have to pass.

As in *The Magic Flute* there are ordeals. Gertrude wins through from the bewildered phase of bereavement, that convulsive nature of grief before which one is powerless, to simply accepting the cruelty of loss. (How Iris, in the happy and productive prime of life could so intimately and imaginatively portray this painful process is remarkable.) The youthful Tim is forced to an equally direct confrontation with his own ingrained untruthfulness, and the consequent falsity hitherto of his whole artistic identity. With his habitual lying, he begins with more of Papageno than Tamino in his temperament, yet finally the implausible marriage of true minds is achieved, as if Papageno were to win the heart of Pamina. Such an astonishing and improbable attraction can only take place within the powerful magic of this enchanted landscape – for in worldly terms it will inevitably appear a grotesque *mesalliance, a coup de foudre* unimaginable in Pimlico.

Ebury Street sees suspicions, confrontations, misunderstandings, subterfuges, offences to civilised morality, interference by well-wishers laden with their own desires and self-deceptions. The world cannot stand still in Ebury Street where all is busy, crowded with incident and governed by clock-time. In the Alpilles the rhythm of seasons, winds, living creatures and the sun sets the pace of the day. It liberates the characters into an access to less conscious yet more urgent feelings, surprising to themselves. After the tragi-comedy of errors in London, with its confusions and hectic clash of egos, the return to the Alpilles where nature imposes its reality seems essential to winning through to truth and trust. Echoes of *The Magic Flute* are everywhere, with its rocky crags and benign wild animals, the test of fidelity through ordeal by water, the admonition to be 'steadfast, patient and silent', the hero's having to accept in silence the perception of the heroine's despair and anguish as in the great G minor aria of Pamina. Gertrude, being like Pamina the stronger character of the two, and knowing the despair both of bereavement and disillusion, nevertheless has waited patiently for the muddles of the metropolis to fall away, before this journey's end in lovers meeting.

There are artists who, without any conscious desire to probe their own psyches, are gifted at allowing their subconscious imagery to take the lead in creating forms. Iris has this natural gift, somehow distinct and apart from intellect, although used in harmony with the implicit morality of the theme. In this she is one of nature's surrealists, though clearly devoid of any conscious intention to observe Surrealist principles. Yet, in observing how her choice of form and elements gathered into her landscape collage in *Nuns and Soldiers* serves to intensify the drama, one can only conjecture how far this creation of a darkly magical *ambience* is involuntary rather than deliberate.

The favourite haunts which Iris and John so enjoyed are in reality widely scattered. They include the rock-pool in the valley below Les Flechons, with its V-shaped cleft, through which the laughing faces of small children from the hamlet above would sometimes appear. It was a happy bathing place for the Bayleys – glowing in brilliant day-light, with its fringe of fern and foliage and a large overhanging tree, but since it is in a hollow, its surface can become as shiny black marble after sunset. Then on the crest of the mountain above it some way to the south a huge stretch of vertical knife edge slabs of stone known as Les Caisses de Servanne enclose a little field, where its excavated roman camp is now hidden under dense maquis. At one point there is a narrow gap in the great rocks, (like a doorway made shiny by the sheep driven past it at Mycenae), through which one could climb to a commanding view of the plain beyond. At yet another point, a long way to the west of Les Caisses, we see from our terrace more giant knife-edge slabs, one of which has a distinct natural configuration of a face. Furthest of all at twenty kilometres away, in the centre of a large town, Salon-de-Provence, there is a tall rocky fountain entirely swathed in moss of a lustrous green which undulates gently as the water trickles down. In the novel, all these elements are gathered together into one small area to form a silent towering space like a natural temple, in which they are made to show their darker aspects. Here the landscape seems to play the stern part of a Sarastro, an intermediary for an unknowable God. It seems to impress the daunting power of nature upon the young hero, newly arrived from the corrupt metropolis, and setting out to find himself. Certainly he at first passes through euphoria at his solitude in paradise, to terror of the faces in the rock and the sinister circular pool, before returning to the terrace of 'Les Saules' where he is surprised to find Gertrude in silent contemplation of the view. The willows appear to represent the softening human proportions within the rocky landscape's assertion of eternity – perhaps even a token of caritas. Stephen and I had planted a weeping willow on the edge of the garden, enjoying its graceful yielding movement as the branches sweep the ground in a Mistral. (Alas, more recently when the plumber insisted on removing its supply of water it inevitably foundered–a group of Tamarisk now similarly respond to the breeze). I imagine that Iris responded intuitively to the genius of the place, the small human habitation enveloped in the majestic implacable landscape, feeling, (and consequently thinking) it to be the powerful theatre in which her morality play will achieve its true and at times sombre significance.

However, the mood of our times together was always sunny, and Stephen and I would listen for the murmur of laughter as John and Iris walked up the lane, returning from their morning bathe. It was the signal for putting the lunch on the table under the mulberry tree. With Stephen they would sometimes talk of work in hand, for instance the Bayleys were both interested and stimulating when Stephen was writing his book on T.S. Eliot, Iris discussing Bradley with her effortless lucidity. Then, I remember a discussion of whether it was credible for Iris' hero to swim through the tunnel of the canal to rescue a drowning dog in *Nuns and Soldiers*. At that time the entrance was obscured by a thick tangle of brambles, and I joked that there was nothing for it but that John should make the attempt. 'Well, do you know, darling? – I don't think I will,' laughed John. A few years later and after publication day, as a result of a forest fire the entrance was entirely cleared. Then with our other guest, Elizabeth Glenconner, they made a formal attempt. I delivered them to the long stretch of the canal on the far side of the rocks, gathered up all their clothes and wraps, drove round the mountain to the parapet where the canal passes under the Maussane road and waited, ready to enfold them in towels after their gruelling escapade. After a very long interval my anxiety dissolved as I saw in the distance all three floating along, waving regally to imaginary spectators on either bank. Although they had not been sure that plausibility was necessary in a fiction, we all felt gratified.

The affection Iris had for animal monsters, the giant lizards for instance, extended also to the human variety, and in her presence, they would bask. For her, 'the Monster' was the friendliest of the pet-names she bestowed, and one who lived up to it was our neighbour, Douglas Cooper, whom she first met with us in 1976. Though he had many friends who understood his volatile nature, its cynicism and virulent hatreds, (no doubt borne of anxiety), could blow up ferociously at any moment making social occasions hazardous. Yet he adored Iris, and she looked forward affectionately to seeing 'the Monster' on every visit. Knowing how he could fuss even loyal friends, save for the imperturbable Basil Amulree, Stephen and I marvelled at his instant serenity and a kind of benign brilliance when in her company, and tried to explain it to each other. We saw that when he started with malicious wit on what promised to be a crescendo of spite and destructiveness about some acquaintance of his, she chuckled a reply which always seemed to make further barbs wither away. We always admired the fact that, despite her views as a moral philosopher being profound and wide-ranging, in personal life she was shiningly unjudgmental. It always seemed that her nature was entirely without a potential for animosity, she simply did not catch the vibes. With that, she was always gifted in appreciating the wholeness of a personality, and by osmosis Douglas seemed aware of her perceptive acceptance, which created at least for the time being an atmosphere of 'La Belle et la Bête'.

Then there were times of great hilarity, as when, entirely to humour
Stephen and me, they joined in our playing 'Scrabble'. There was no hint of
competitive game-playing, Iris could not begin to calculate or remotely to
care about scoring. But they were delighted by the random occurrence of
dotty words as they shuffled their letters. 'Oh do look, pussy, – BUNFISH!'
was the exclamation. There would follow an inspired improvisation
whereby the word seemed to acquire an illusion of meaning, yet remaining
resistant to definition; it flitted through the conversation like *fern follets*.
The frivolous fantasy taking possession of the serious philosopher and the
literary critic was always irresistible.

In our waterless years when our household supply had to be measured
in cupfuls, we were visited one evening by a water diviner who said that
there was a vein of water, not very deep, in the olive orchard below the
house. We wandered down, drinks in hand to watch as he slowly walked
a line across the terrain. At a certain point, whichever the direction of his
straight path, the willow wand, horizontally taut between his hands, would
rise into the vertical. He persuaded us to try, but I declined, knowing that
my lack of talent would dash our hopes. Both Stephen and Iris turned out
to be magically endowed as diviners; at the very spot the wand sprang
out of Iris' hand. 'Madame a la fluide,' said the diviner with an evident
reverence and Stephen had remarked that whatever the sign under which
they are born, 'all poets are Pisceans'. The scene made a huge dent in my
scepticism, augmented when later a vein was found below that exact spot.
The incident was yet another small sign of Iris living in that perfect balance
desired by Jungians between intuition and intellect

In friendship, this shows itself in the balance between empathy
and intelligence which is wisdom. It appeals to those of contrasting
temperament or views. A long-standing professional friend who loved
and respected her was A. J. Ayer. During his last illness in 1988, Freddie,
looking frail but cheerful, with his wife Dee and son Nicolas joined us one
summer's day, for a long lunch in Aix-en- Provence. Alone at an open-air
cafe with Iris, he told her about his 'out-of-the-body' experience when in
a recent crisis at the hospital he had for a short interval been effectively
dead. It had changed his awareness in many ways, and he was reluctant
to talk of it to others except in a superficial almost joking way by which
the inexplicable is kept at bay. But in Iris he was sure of that blend of
sensitivity and intelligence which he would not feel crassly challenging. As
the rest of us strolled towards them, we perceived an unusual atmosphere,

concentrated, serene, intent, yet expansive – without pressure, as if some indefinable quandary had dissolved.

This year, 1998, as always Iris and John came to stay – this time accompanied by Peter Conradi. The onslaught of her present condition upon her memory must be a nightmare, so that my modest hopes were only for some small vestige of familiarity from past years to survive enough to give her pleasure and reassurance. In England it is almost impossible to imagine the extent of bewilderment she must suffer in memory loss, which lies behind her frequently repeated, questions about where she is – 'What is this place?' That question seemed only to occur at the railway station in Avignon. At Saint Jerome we enjoyed revisiting all the old haunts which had inspired *Nuns and Soldiers*, and a sense of timeless shared affection for these sites somehow alleviated the lack of Stephen's presence. To see Iris and John pottering off down the lane as always faithfully followed by Daisy the cat, and deep in conversation where the lack of usual sense or reference is entirely unimportant, gave assurance of their transcendence over her affliction – a disturbance on the surface of the mind which cannot touch their close devotion. It was a very happy time. On her arrival in our valley she had said with dawning pleasure, 'Oh, this is MY place!'

And so, as it lives in the book, it always will be.

Iris Murdoch:
A Letter from India

Saguna Ramanathan

How does one begin to write of an effect so profound as to change, if anything can, the core of one's thought and action, and help one to grow in 'grace and wisdom'? Or how does one trace the trajectory of a relationship which grew and grew under my wondering, astonished and grateful eyes? What process was at work when, across the miles separating continent from continent, books and letters established a contact between an obscure academic and a world-famous writer?

I first started reading Iris Murdoch in 1967, borrowing volumes from the public library in Ahmedabad –*A Severed Head* and *The Bell* and *Under the Net*. There followed a period of no Murdoch at all – I had exhausted whatever the library had, and my interests lay elsewhere; I was bringing up my children. And then, a book called *A Word Child* came into my hands. The former English cricket captain, Mike Brearley, connected with Ahmedabad through marriage (I have never met him), gave the book which he recommended highly to a young friend of mine, and she lent it to me. As I read on, amazed and troubled, I came to the part where Hilary is in the church in which Eliot used to pray. The final paragraph of that section hit me as if with a sword. Here was a writer, I realized, who was making me rethink all my categories anew, a different Iris Murdoch, it seemed, from the one I remembered, different from anything I had ever read, speaking, it seemed, the truth about the truth, that shifting complexity which alone can be called the truth, if indeed there is any such thing. I was caught; it was an experience that only deepened with every subsequent novel: I hungered for more. To one who was embarked on a search, here was the most extraordinary guide and companion.

I wrote to her in 1979, by which time I had devoured everything possible; and true to her scrupulous way of answering all correspondence, she replied, taking my questions seriously. I am not sure how, or exactly when, it changed from a formal to an affectionate note – perhaps when, in reply to a letter written in 1984 about a re-reading of *Henry and Cato*, she dropped all the honorifics, and wrote quite simply, 'My dear Suguna, what a wonderful letter: it gave me the greatest possible pleasure.' I knew that what I had been saying had been picked up absolutely accurately and perfectly.

My meeting in 1987 with Iris in her Oxford home was remarkable for my ineptitude and her warmth. I was early, as I invariably am for any appointment, and stood waiting under a tree outside her house, unaware that she had seen me from her window but was not quite sure whether I was the same person from India who had asked for a meeting. I fumbled and asked stupid questions, I had no camera and no tape recorder, and now when I look back at my notes, I think I wasted a splendid opportunity. But that is not altogether true, because I was taking in this person in quite other ways. She was so kind; that legendary kindness was astonishing. When I said I wanted to go to Spain, she offered me money in case I needed it – from which incredibly generous gesture my middle-class soul shrank back in horror. But she asked me to go back and visit her the next day with the litany of the Virgin of Loretto which I happened to have mentioned. She read it aloud in the Anglicised Latin pronunciation unfamiliar to me, thanked me for it, and asked me about myself. When I showed her a picture of my husband with our pet beagle, she exclaimed, 'What a marvellous dog! I should be saying what a marvellous husband – that too!!'

Her advice to me, as to many others, was that I should write my own novel. We talked about many things, and clearly she was deeply interested in India's spiritual inheritance. She appeared to think that I was lucky to have it in the background while immersed in a Western setting (choice of subject) and Christian institution (place of work). I could not quite see what she meant. It seemed to me that I was caught between the two: robbed of my own by the accidents of history, and incapable of belonging to the other by accident of birth.

But we talked comfortably and sporadically. She told me that she was still romantically in love with her husband, and asked me about myself. I found that I was talking about myself rather than getting her to make pronouncements for the article I never wrote. I never wrote it simply because I could not catch in the net of my consciousness a person so varied, wise, intelligent, and compassionate. What could be possibly said about that absence of self-regard without dramatising and falsifying it?

We continued to write to each other twice or thrice a year. She asked me once to put my address on every letter in case she ever lost it. And she wrote appreciatively about my study of goodness in her later novels. But when I sent her a paper on religion using the terms of contemporary critical theory, she disapproved of the language of deconstruction, and told me in no uncertain terms that it was arcane and unnecessary. The surprising thing about the interaction was that one was taken seriously; one was treated as a friend. A letter begins 'My dear girl' and all letters after the 1980s end with 'much love'. Is one making too much of it? I believe not. If she was communicating warmth it was because she felt it. If her novels made me think about life, her letters made me feel happy with myself.

I cannot bear to open the packet of her letters now, but I believe that it was some time in 1995 that she wrote to say that she was feeling exhausted. There was another in which she said about *Metaphysics as a Guide to Morals*, 'It's a bit chaotic, I'm afraid'. And then 1996 and silence. And then a tiny news report in the *Times of India* that Dame Iris Murdoch was suffering from writers' block; and another a little later, in which she was reported as saying that 'the whole thing had packed up and gone'. I could make nothing of it till I heard from a friend that she had heard that Iris had been diagnosed with Alzheimer's disease.

Iris and the Theatre

Josephine Hart

Hugely pregnant I almost stumbled into The Connaught, racing to meet an author who had years ago, in a sense, stolen my mind. Dazzled by her novel *The Black Prince* I wanted to produce it as a play.

Iris Murdoch, an intensely physical presence, sat in one of the very grand chairs in that very grand lounge smiling calmly, quietly at me as I approached. She was dressed in what I later learned was her favourite colour blue, which stongly emphasized the cornflower blue of her eyes. The Irish have a theory about pale blue eyes

'I'm Irish, too', she said. A point through our treasured friendship which she was to make often. Iris has a steady way of gazing at the person to whom she speaks, which combined with the sturdy completeness of her figure, is both arresting and calming. It's as though she is saying 'Rest, just for a moment, rest and think'.

We had a four hour lunch. She spoke to me with such directness and wisdom I felt as though she knew something about me which I myself didn't quite understand. She spoke of her own life – of the war and its aftermath and, at one point, I wept. I had the most complete conversation I have ever had in my life. It was as though we shared in those hours what Yeats once described as 'the awful gift of intimacy'. It was not so much that it was private conversation – it was almost secret and it had a profound effect on me. From that day I have loved Iris in a way, which, apart from my family, I have loved no one else.

Her novels, which first drew her to me, are of course thrillingly clever witty exciting and often shocking. They have translated wonderfully onto stage and into film. But their great enduring power lies beyond that. She is the novelist who guides the reader down the labyrinthine paths of their own minds – where sudden terrors, or conversely, shafts of insight may change everything or nothing. She looks full-face at sin and frighteningly at its redemptive after-shocks. She writes of the entwining of Eros and Thanatos and warns us of 'the false pair and the true pair'. That Eros is also the God of Art she makes clear in *The Black Prince*, and that writing is a small gift one lays before him. This 'humility in all things' is something she shares with Eliot and is, perhaps, a truer mark of greatness than many modem writers realise.

But she is also the person who has taught me that surrender of the ego can lie happily side by side with the realisation of the self. And that the realisation of self – so prized in our time – is predicated on the deepest respect for the reality of others. This aspect of Iris' character is at its most moving in the grave sweetness with which she listens to children, the wholly genuine attention she gives to their comments and the care with which she answers their questions. This profound gracefulness towards other people is I think one of the reasons she is – though I know she dislikes it – so often described as good.

Iris' voyage has been magnificent. The islands she discovered and mapped out for us are deeply precious in that within their sanctuary we can know ourselves better.

Painting Iris Murdoch

Tom Phillips

The picture was painted in the usual corner of my studio in Peckham. Iris is sitting in my usual sitter's chair, half looking out of the window: sometimes, if intriguing people passed by, or dogs (a liking for which we do not share), she would lean out of position to get a better look. Since Iris lives in Oxford and comes to London only for the occasional crowded day or two, sittings were irregular. The work in fact spanned three years and involved about fifteen sittings in all, each lasting a couple of hours or so with a break or two for coffee.

When I first met Iris (at a dinner party given by Michael Kustow) we talked about Titian's *Flaying of Marsyas* which we had both just seen at the magnificent Venice exhibition at the Royal Academy. When the National Portrait Gallery commissioned me to paint her portrait I recalled our conversation (about whom we each most identified with in the picture) and started a fairly hasty copy of the picture to act as a backdrop so that she might sit with her own head in front of the head of Marsyas. My original image of Iris was quickly formed. She has a luminous presence and the visual metaphor [for her] that came into my mind was of an electric light bulb in that gloomy corner, glowing, casting out darkness. I suppose this is what people of a mystical bent call an 'aura'.

Unfortunately, on the canvas itself I lost this vision about half way through the work. Iris started to shrink and began to lose heavily to the Titian. Taking advantage of a longish break, I thought hard about how to get out of this impasse without faking. By her next visit I had started from memory four very large drawings whose scale challenged the painting. Each one of the drawings seemed to deal with a different element and I came to think of them as representing earth, air, fire, and water. In more practical terms they taught me that the historiated aspects of Iris' face, its lines and creases, were not really important to her actual presence. Thus, I found my way back to the original light-bulb image.

I am more at home with Iris Murdoch's books of philosophy than with her novels, perhaps because she often speaks of (and, here and there, directly to), the artist: she deals so clearly with Plato's Theory of Forms that via her I have for the first time really grasped some of the implications for my own activity. In a hazy and untutored way, the portrait is also a type of dialogue. Three modes of representation are present: in the painting of the face itself there is a precarious balance between painting what I see and what I know in order to make a permanent image from transient perceptions; the picture in the background is distanced by already being a copy of a copy of a copy of the original, yet paradoxically it is the most naturalistically painted thing in the portrait based on pure observation of the effect of light on the object before me; the plant represents a third kind of treatment objectivity.

Right from the start I had wanted a 'bit of nature' to be present. In all her novels Iris Murdoch suddenly flings open the windows of Hampstead or the Gloucester Road and through some wangle of the plot – Five Go Off to a Sanatorium – some of the characters escape to the countryside which enables the writer to show her unrivalled sympathy with the world of living things, especially the plants of the English hedgerows. To have featured an Iris would have been too dumb. At our second sitting I made a wild guess and suggested a gingko, and it turned out that we were both enthusiasts for the world's oldest tree. Luckily there is a fine specimen in my own garden and towards the end of the sittings I therefore put in a gingko branch, painted in the manner of old botanical illustrations. I first made a separate study of it in case it might die. In the end, the branch in the picture was painted directly from nature though slightly adapted to rhyme with other elements in the painting, like the collar, and the arm of Apollo. Once the plant was in and doing its work the picture was finished with only the nerve-racking business of varnishing left. This is a moment of truth when all the dried paint suddenly springs back to life and the harmonies of the picture, guessed at from stage to stage as wet paint was applied to over dry, are revealed. All was well.

When as in this case a well-loved national institution is painted for a National Institution, the work tends to receive some publicity and critical attention. A mixed reception is always invigorating and none could have been more varied than that provoked by this particular portrait, ranging as it did from Waldemar Januszczak in the *Guardian* who wrote:

> Her head glows like a light... behind it a detail from Titian... shows one of Apollo's acolytes scraping the skin of Marsyas' body, revealing raw flesh, just as a good Iris Murdoch narrative scrapes away the surface of ordinary life to reveal the questioning agonies and rousing passions underneath. This is not just a fine likeness it is also a portrait of an inner life. It is the show's notable success, a work of obvious thoughtfulness and ambition. Phillips manages to endow this... middle-aged Englishwoman with the dignity of a Venetian Doge.

to Brian Sewell in the *Evening Standard*, who commented characteristically:

> by far the most deplorable new acquisition is Tom Phillips' portrait of Iris Murdoch. It is accompanied by bewildering preparatory material. There is a frankly appalling copy of Titian that would have been better done in chalk by a pavement artist outside the Gallery. There are huge hideous and wilfully distorted drawings of the novelist herself, out of focus, with the complexion of flaking distemper... an inoffensive study of a Gingko leaf... more plastic than real. And all these are brought together in dreadful disunity in the final portrait where poor jaundice-eyed Miss Murdoch is as flat and grainy as an overblown holiday snap. Could none of the trustees see how bad it is? Did none of them want to reject it?

Fortunately, Sewell was in the minority and, most important of all, the sitter herself said wonderfully encouraging things about the work.

The after-life of the picture has also been eventful. It was the first work of art published in colour in the then newly launched *Independent* and the National Portrait Gallery made a postcard of it (Iris had always wanted to become a postcard). It made a tour of Britain with its attendant studies. I kept on getting invitations to various venues like Gainsborough's House where it had taken up residence for a while. I could not resist one of these when I read the card in which the Ulster Museum invited me to attend a 'Private View of the portrait of IRISH MURDOCH by Tom Phillips'.

I think we both enjoyed working on the painting; as ever such a task is in the end a partnership and Iris was always interested in its progress as well as how the rest of the work was developing in the studio. We had much good conversation and many laughs. I cannot now remember what prompted Iris to persuade me to sing my old school song ('Still Henry Thornton's known for labours philanthropic / He loosened slavery's chains throughout the sultry tropic...') or what gave rise to her singing (in her fine contralto voice) a socialist rally chorus in the middle of another sitting.

On one occasion, I rashly criticised the covers of the hardback versions of her novels and found myself thereby gently trapped into designing thereafter them forever after (three so far and always each year a new one on the way). Thus, in one form our collaboration continues long after the sitter is gone and the portrait ended and I have a good alibi for reading whopper novels with great delight.

Postscript

Our friendship survived the business of a portrait and we met and corresponded with that infrequent regularity which hardworking artists favour. Our last proper meeting was in 1995 when I introduced my wife-to-be, Fiona, to Iris at The Ivy. She had many memories of the restaurant in its former glory but was already showing signs of confusion. I would then only see her at St Catherine's Feasts being looked after by John with robust tenderness. On the last of these occasions I was touched when on being (so to speak) reintroduced to me by John, Iris said, 'Of course I know you, you are in a famous painting... in a portrait.' All the old radiance came into her face and I saw again the luminous beauty that had made me want to paint her years before.

Encounters with Iris Murdoch

Cheryl Bove

My life-long interest in Iris Murdoch and her works began as an undergraduate in 1965. The instructor of my contemporary British novel seminar had recently returned from England (by boat) bringing back Penguin paperbacks (then unavailable for sale in the U.S. due to copyright reasons) of such authors as Anthony Powell, John Barth, Malcolm Bradbury and Iris Murdoch for the seminar. We read *The Bell* in class, and Murdoch appealed to me because of the depth in her work and because I had a philosophy minor. Our professor encouraged us to choose one of these emerging writers to follow throughout their careers, reading everything we could by and about them. This practice led, years later, to assisting J.W.J. Fletcher and co-editing Iris Murdoch: *A Descriptive Primary and Annotated Secondary Bibliography for Garland*.

At an early stage in my studies I hesitated to contact Iris and did not realize how generous she was with her time, kindly responding to anyone who wrote to her. After I met her we did correspond, though rarely, because of my feeling that she must have experienced what was evident in her novels: the pull between otherness and art. The good artist should have time for others and yet such distractions as letters from the general public must detract from her time for her art. This concern became the basis of some conversations that we did have, branching into the issue of whether being a flawed person would necessarily detract from the artist's vision–she cited the example of D.H. Lawrence in saying that she did not feel that that was always necessarily so.

It was frustrating not to find an eager and receptive audience for Murdoch's aesthetics in America because she was not a feminist at a time when Feminism was in full sway in American universities. Iris' remarks suggesting that studying classes of novels such as 'feminist novels' would mean overlooking some of the best novels led to her own novels being left off syllabi. Though her philosophy was more acceptable, her novels were not popular in politically charged universities. Even so, students read them enthusiastically in my humanities classes and colleagues taught them in their classes.

Two meetings with Iris stand out in my memories, the first and the last. We met for the first time in 1985 at an International Conference in Amsterdam. Iris and John Bayley sat at a table near the speakers' podium and responded to five of the conference papers, including mine, which, in part, regretted that some of her least attractive characters ended up in America. Following the paper, Iris laughed and said something to the effect of, 'Well I think I have to defend myself; I loved Berkeley and always thought that placing my characters in America was giving them a new beginning.'

Talking with her was probably a similar experience for many who interviewed her throughout the years. She usually asked, 'Do you believe in God and, if so, how formally?' She clearly had an interest in unusual religious beliefs, even famously describing herself as a 'sort of Christian-Buddhist.' Her oft-repeated question must have been formed by this interest. I once interviewed one of her friends, a bookseller who lived in the chaplain's house of an Oxford Anglican convent. He related that she had asked him to invite several Oxford clerics to lunch – particularly those with unorthodox beliefs, including an Oxford chaplain who did not believe in the Virgin birth – because she was interested in their views. Some of these clerics surely formed the basis for characters such as Carel Fisher (*The Time of the Angels*) and the unnamed demythologizing bishops mentioned in *The Book and the Brotherhood*.

The last time I talked with Iris was during an exchange semester at Oxford. I asked John and Iris to join two friends and myself for dinner at the Randolph hotel. Barbara Phillips (a senior civil servant) and Glynn Phillips (a philosopher) seemingly would have interested the Bayleys. Glynn and Barbara are vegetarians, and we were having drinks in the bar while waiting for our table when Barbara remarked how pleased she was to learn that the Randolph offered three vegetarian main choices, unusual for the 1990s time period. We went on to discuss the ethics of eating animals, and Iris was agreeing with the merits of Barbara's position just as the waiter came around to ask us for our dinner orders. Iris smiled and quickly said, 'Nevertheless, I'll have beef.' Much of that dinner conversation turned to Oxford writers, and John asked if we had read Barbara Pym. We had, so he told us about some of her Oxford exploits and mentioned that she was buried in Holy Trinity churchyard in Finstock, the church where T.S. Eliot was received into the Anglican Church. The next day Barbara and I located the church and found Barbara Pym's grave sadly overgrown with tall grasses.

My rewarding and lasting memories of Iris will always include meeting and working with so many Murdoch scholars from around the world who also exhibit the generosity of spirit that so became Iris. Editing the *Iris Murdoch Newsletter* allowed me the opportunity to correspond with and become aware of the scholars writing in Murdoch studies.

Relaxing with Iris and John

Audi Bayley

When I first met Iris I was quite new to Oxford, but already used to the fact that few people took any notice of me the moment they discovered that I had no 'subject'. I also soon learnt not to approach anybody I had not been introduced to, as I as often as not was given a cold shoulder.

Parties, specially drinks, were a nightmare as I was usually left on my own with nobody to talk to. I was therefore immensely flattered when Iris (we had been introduced on a previous occasion) whom I had admired very much having read her both in English and in Norwegian translation, took pity upon me and approached me at a party in 1966 or 67. Her opening words were as follows: 'How nice to see you dear girl, do you believe in God?' I ought not to have been surprised considering how important religion is in her books. But coming from a country where people still believed in Hell, and where God was, and still is, regarded far too personal a matter to be discussed with anybody but your very closest friends, I was slightly taken aback and at the same time rather amused.

My answer was in the affirmative which seemed to please her. We talked a bit about religion and were then called to the table. After dinner I was grilled again, this time about my relationship with my parents and my brothers; were they all alive, did I love them, how much did I love them, and so on, little did I know then that this was the beginning of what was to become a long and close friendship.

I have since learnt that religion and morals play an extraordinarily important part, not only in her books, but to an even greater extent in her personal life and conduct. It is a subject we would often return to in the early hours of the morning when we would all be getting increasingly muddled after a long and leisurely dinner with a lot to drink, and I dare say made very little sense. Iris would then suddenly take charge, and with authority and a few words put us back on the right track, so sure is she of herself in this respect that I cannot remember anybody trying to argue with her.

There have been many trips abroad, mostly to Italy where we explored the North, the South and the Centre. Iris and John are, as would be expected, the most enchanting travel companions, always alert and interested, noticing everything and making relevant and amusing observations. Iris would carry little pieces of paper in order to jot down things that caught her eye, including moods and impressions. Often she would run out, and there would be a scramble between the four of us for another scrap of paper. It became an amusing game to read her novels and spot the references. It would often be things we had talked about or things we had seen, or done together.

One of our experiences, which she put into *The Green Knight* about the *passeggiata* in the square of a little town 'somewhere in the Apennines', actually took place in Ascoli Piceno, a lovely medieval town, little visited, near the Adriatic. Iris and I spent what seemed like an eternity walking arm-in-arm round and round the square among a dense crowd of good-natured Italians of all ages, surrendering ourselves, and becoming one with the mass of people. Meanwhile we were being watched by John and Borys who, having found it all too claustrophobic, had retired to an open–air café.

The bridge scene from the same novel comes from Spoleto where Iris refused to cross it. I think the place frightened her and she makes it an important episode in young Harvey's life. She has this wonderful gift of description, rereading something, often a long time afterwards, brings it all back so vividly.

Iris and John would come and stay with us, now unfortunately only me, since Borys sadly died in 1992. Their arrival was an event always eagerly anticipated. One knows that one shall have a most interesting and amusing fortnight including, as often as not, some island hopping. Lanzarote is wonderful for swimming and it is still possible to find virtually deserted sandy beaches with crystal clear water. However, pebbled beaches, where it can often be quite difficult to get in or out of the water, are preferred. Pebbled beaches offer one advantage though; we all like collecting stones, and quite a happy time can be had by all pursuing this activity.

I used to have a beautiful grey pebble with a purple stripe which I had treasured for years. I offered it to Iris who refused to accept it. Just as they were leaving for England I put it in her hand luggage without telling her. I never heard a word and thought it must have fallen out of the bag, it being an open one. It was not until a couple of years later that it appears no less that three times in *The Book and The Brotherhood*! Needless to say I was very touched.

Weather permitting, not a day will pass without an excursion to the beach or a trip on the boat. Iris swimming in her 'Greek swimming dress', and John as often as not in his clothes, including his cap. Snorkelling is a favoured activity, and fishes are much admired, which makes for difficulties at 'Pedro's' our fish restaurant. We will see the boat coming in with the newly caught fish which is then cleaned on the rocks not far from our table before being prepared and served. Horror of horrors; Iris refuses to touch the stuff and orders scrambled eggs and a salad.

Being the most considerate of guests they will usually get up as quiet as mice and make themselves a cup of tea about half-past seven in the morning. Then they work to nine when we will have breakfast, and then there is more work to be done until about midday when it is time for a drink and an outing to the beach to have a look at the fishes before lunch, which is often long and wet. Home for a rest, possibly some more work and then there is time for drinks/dinner.

Iris uses our study to write in behind closed doors. During a visit I noticed that our favourite cat 'Stalky' disappeared for several hours every morning. It turned out she was sitting on the desk, like an Egyptian cat, watching Iris write. Being afraid that the cat disturbed her, I told Iris to throw her out. 'I like her there' came the answer. 'She has a calming effect on me, and makes me concentrate.

John, who is not particularly fond of cats, would often find himself with 'Stalky' on his lap the moment he sat down. Thinking this was cats' usual way of imposing themselves upon the person who least likes them, we paid little notice, until one day I saw the cat putting her paw into John's pocket and fishing out some bit of food which she then proceeded to eat, then back with her paw for another bit. He couldn't understand our sudden merriment and we discretely didn't tell him. 'Stalky' appears briefly in *The Good Apprentice*.

On one of their early visits, there being few direct charter flights to Lanzarote, John and Iris flew out via Span and Gran Canary. On their return we accompanied them to Las Palmas where they had to spend the night in order to catch the plane at 7 a.m. the following morning.

We went out to dinner with several of our Spanish friends, one of whom had brought a pretty, shy-looking Oriental girl with no make-up, waring glasses and a dark brown velvet suit with a high-necked white blouse. I was chatting to this girl before dinner when Iris joined us. Their conversation went as follows:

'Where do you come from?'
'From Seoul.'
'How interesting, such a fascinating place. I have been there with my husband. Are you here on holiday?'
'No, I work here.'
'What kind of work?'
'I dance.'
'Oh, you must be part of a group performing traditional dances.'
'No, I dance alone.'
'Do you, then you must be very talented. Do you wear beautiful national costume?'
'No, I strip.'

End of conversation. Of course Iris had to make one of her characters into a stripper. After dinner we went dancing till five in the morning and then straight to the airport not having slept in our beautiful rooms overlooking the beach.

John, not being a great friend of London, would often stay in Oxford while we took Iris out to a meal or similar. On one occasion we asked them to [the Royal Opera House at Covent Garden to see *Eugene Onegin*. John politely declined saying he was not very fond of opera, indeed had little interest in it. It was a good production with Thomas Allen as Onegin and Ileana Cortubas as Tatyanya, and Iris was crying throughout. It was not till the next morning when I read the programme that I discovered that John had written the main piece.

How typical! They are both such modest persons. Iris has always been most reluctant to discuss her own books, which have given us so much pleasure. Each new novel being awaited with great excitement. But she is always ready to discuss literature on a general level, and wonderfully interesting and illuminating discussions they have been.

When we couldn't see each other, Borys, who was a bad sleeper, wrote Iri long letters about his childhood and all sorts of things in the middle of the night. A flourishing correspondence developed which gave him immense pleasure.

Iris' wisdom and insight and above all her uncanny sixth sense has always been a marvel to me, as well as her truthfulness and goodness. Of her characteristics her saintliness is what I most admire. After thirty years of friendship I have never heard her utter a disparaging remark about anybody. It would be difficult if not impossible to find a more positive person. As we know from her books, she certainly knows about evil, but it plays no part whatsoever in her own life.

Time passes only too quickly in their company. They always leave a great void when they depart, there is only the memory of the most rewarding time left. Except on one occasion when we found two hard boiled eggs in the electric kettle when they were already back in England.

A Memoir of Iris

Paul Levy

It's difficult to remember when I first met Iris and John – in my experience, they were inseparable. I am certain we met in the late summer of 1968 at the Oxford house in Charlbury Road of Lord and Lady David Cecil – though it's just possible that we had met earlier, in 1963, with a gaggle of Oxford philosophers at a party at Edith Grove, World's End, in Chelsea. David and Rachel Cecil considered themselves in loco parentis to me; I had only just returned to England on a Harvard Travelling Fellowship, leaving behind their middle child, Hugh, my best friend, whose Harkness Fellowship had one more term to go. Alongside the unselfconscious traces of the beauty she had been when younger, the impression Iris made in the 1960s was of a strong person with some softer edges, someone who – was I surprised, having read all her novels? – was relaxed, and good at small talk. (One of the signs of her dementia was that she began conversations with a regal 'Have you come far?', and repeated the question after an alarmingly short interval.) John and Iris were close to David and Rachel Cecil; John was David's pupil, as well as his successor at New College. Iris liked a glass or two, and a joke. The Cecil's cook, Olive, was adequate rather than accomplished; once that autumn, Rachel seated me next to Iris at dinner. I was fiddling a bit with my plate; Iris noticed, and asked, in a subtle way, if something was wrong. I whispered that I was finding the chicken a bit difficult to cut up. 'That's because it's Olive's pheasant,' smiled Iris, who did not cook at all. (In my *Independent* obituary I wrote: 'Iris was not much of a cook, though she was proud of her *stifado*, a Greek dish of beef, olives, tomatoes, wine and vinegar.' I cannot imagine where I got that nugget – I can't recall a single morsel of food cooked by Iris.)

After David arranged a place for me at Oxford the following year, the Bayleys and I saw a good deal of each other, at Cedar Lodge, Steeple Aston or during weekends at the Cecil's Red Lion House in Dorset. Though I was nominally a DPhil Student at Nuffield College, I was in truth a PhD

candidate at Harvard, and indeed already had a contract for my book on
G.E. Moore and the Cambridge Apostles, which I submitted in lieu of a
dissertation. Iris took a genuine interest in this, right from its beginnings; I
managed to procrastinate for nearly ten years, but Iris read the chapters as
I painfully produced them, and then the entire typescript, even writing a
generous, long, 'selling' puff for the dust-jacket.

When I moved to the beautiful 17th century Yarnton Manor in 1971, only
a few miles from Oxford, I could at last return hospitality to Iris and John,
who had known the place when it was owned by George Kolkhorst. Its
website says Iris visited as part of a touring theatre troupe, which I had
not known; in the three years I lived there, with Joel Fadem, my Oxford
housemate, and Penelope Marcus, my wife-to-be, we had some regular
fixtures with John and Iris. Every Easter we lunched or dined and then
played charades, dumb crambo, sardines or murder. Were John and Iris the
most senior guests? I don't think so, as I can remember Frances Partridge
being with us – but Iris took part with gusto. One Easter, the other tenants
having moved, we briefly had possession of the entire house, and there was
a game of sardines in which Iris joined the other players on a bathroom
window-ledge at least ten feet above the bathtub. There was no ladder in
evidence; she must have been hauled up by the others, with someone in
the bath assisting. Iris could get angry – a foolish remark about Ireland
or Irish politics always lit a very short fuse – but she adored the odd bout
of silliness, and would lift her chin, grin and throw her short hair back in
glee.

After another such lunch, all of us having drunk too deeply, someone
mentioned that Garsington Manor, the former home of Lady Ottoline
Morrell and the Bloomsbury Group's favourite resort, was opening its
gardens for charity, so we piled into a car, arrived, paid our pound or two
entrance fee, and marvelled at the Italian garden and the pond. On the
way out, John suddenly recalled that he knew the owners, the Wheeler-
Bennetts, and he knocked on the door near the loggia. When there was no
reply, he knocked more vigorously, eventually banging his feet as well as
his hands. Lady Wheeler-Bennett opened the door to John, as the rest of us
made our blushing excuses and tried to dissolve into the shrubbery.

You could just about imagine swimming in the algae-covered tank-thing at
Steeple Aston, but it became difficult to eat comfortably, once you had seen
the second kitchen's sink, full of coppery pots and pans turning the water

blue-green. John did all the cooking, and Iris was full of praise for his skills and imagination. She was quick to say that John was the best cook she'd ever known, and claimed she had endowed Charles Arrowby in *The Sea, The Sea* with John's 'culinary talent.' Actually, Arrowby cooks horrifyingly disgusting meals for himself (the menus were, they both said, suggested by John, who would shock people by pretending to find the food perfectly nice).

In the early 1980s Iris asked me to explain the French nouvelle cuisine movement (I was food & wine editor of *The Observer*), and when I came to the emphasis on novel ingredients and pairings, she said it was just as she had suspected, John had got there first. It was true that he did unexpected things with kippers. Iris seemed to enjoy meals in our foodie household – she had, after all, been a guest at the 1984 Dorchester Hotel launch of *The Official Foodie Handbook* by Ann Barr and me, and she radiated joy, sitting at my table, with Terence Conran on one side of her, and Pierre Troisgros on the other. The concept was a touch alien to her, but she saw the fun of the whole business, and appreciated Anton Mosimann's creation of the seafood sausage filled with oysters, scallops and lobster, though she probably couldn't have described it the next day. In 1985 we managed to give lunch to 20-odd people in our kitchen, for an occasion called 'doctors wear scarlet,' celebrating the simultaneous honorary D.Litts London given to Iris and to the artist, Howard Hodgkin.

Iris was a superb hostess, filling the drawing room at Steeple Aston with three or four round tables, and taking a lot of trouble with the *place à table*. She and John took pleasure in arranging things so that you sat, not necessarily with old friends, but with someone whose company you would relish. At Steeple Aston you might be introduced, and sit next to at a meal: Antony and Lady Violet Powell; J.B. Priestley and Jacquetta Hawkes; Roy and Jennifer Jenkins; Philippa Foot; Isaiah and Aline Berlin; Asa Briggs; Patrick and Susan Gardiner, Stuart Hampshire, Herbert and Jennifer Hart, Denis and Edna Healey; David and Anne Pears; Tony and Marcelle Quinton; Peter and Ann Strawson; Noel and Gaby Annan; Janet Stone; Anthony and Catherine Storr; Rachel Trickett; or Borys and Audi Villers. There was not a trace of snobbery in either John or Iris; indeed, John assumed that everyone knew everyone else. Once at lunch there in late 1973, John had been on the phone in the room just off the drawing room, and told me he was being consulted about a collection of memories of W.H. Auden's last days at Oxford. 'You should be writing something for it,' said John spontaneously. He could scarcely credit my saying that I'd never even encountered Auden.

In 1981, Iris agreed to be an atheist godmother to our first daughter, Tatyana, which unorthodox role she carried out with imagination. She had a much senior godson, the Times columnist and superb spy-story writer, Ben MacIntyre; and I think I also remember an African godchild. She gave imaginative presents – a gold bracelet too heavy for the slight Tatyana to wear, and copies of her books at appropriate junctures of childhood and adolescence. Iris even came to see Tatyana in the Dragon School play. Was it Iris, or did John give me the not quite oval, oversized, glittering, grey pebble, streaked and veined with white marble, weighing 615g and about 11cm diameter? It is fairly smooth, polished only by years of handling it, while it sat on her writing table.

A terrible taste of what was to come was the Cheltenham Literary Festival in 1994. John elected to drive, which was itself a memorable event; though despite him looking more often at the back-seat passenger (me) than at the road, he was a perfectly safe driver. It was at dinner that night that I realised that Iris' increasing vagueness was slipping over into dementia, as she returned repeatedly to the same topics. Ralph Steadman was artist-in-residence for the 1994 Festival, and did portraits of all the chief speakers. In a touching post-script to the *Guardian* obituary [10 Feb 1999], he wrote: 'They shuffled in like bewildered refugees. Iris Murdoch was dishevelled and childlike and John Bayley was attentive and concerned. I was not aware of her condition and, fearful of charging my memory with false impressions, I would say that she enjoyed our encounter as a child would enjoy a game, which of course it was.' John and Iris were advertised as having a 'conversation,' which had attracted a huge audience. No one seemed to notice that while their questions were directed to Iris, John fielded every single one of them – in an unselfconscious manner so skilful that you couldn't tell that Iris had scarcely spoken.

There were some bad times, as when Iris would quietly slip out the front door of the North Oxford house to which they'd moved when they left Steeple Aston, and wander, in the way so many Alzheimers's patients do. That she always got safely home is a tribute to the alertness and kindness of the neighbours. Eventually Iris had to go to the wonderful Oxford care home where she, literally, turned her face to the wall and died. Penny and I were at the home with Iris on the day of her death, doing what we could to keep her lips moist; John was staying in Wales with Peter Conradi, Iris' biographer. It was a great relief when we heard John's voice, talking to a nurse in the corridor; for Iris died soon after. Later that evening, I was trying both to write the obituary of Iris and to prepare supper for John, Peter and us. We decided the writing would have to wait, and with a bottle or two, we sat round as Peter played the piano and, prompted by John, sang songs for Iris.

There was a touching postscript when the 2001 movie *Iris* was filming in Oxford; Penny happened to pass, and saw Judi Dench in costume. Penny managed to get word to the wardrobe mistress that she would be glad to help by lending some of Iris' own clothes, which she had been given by John.

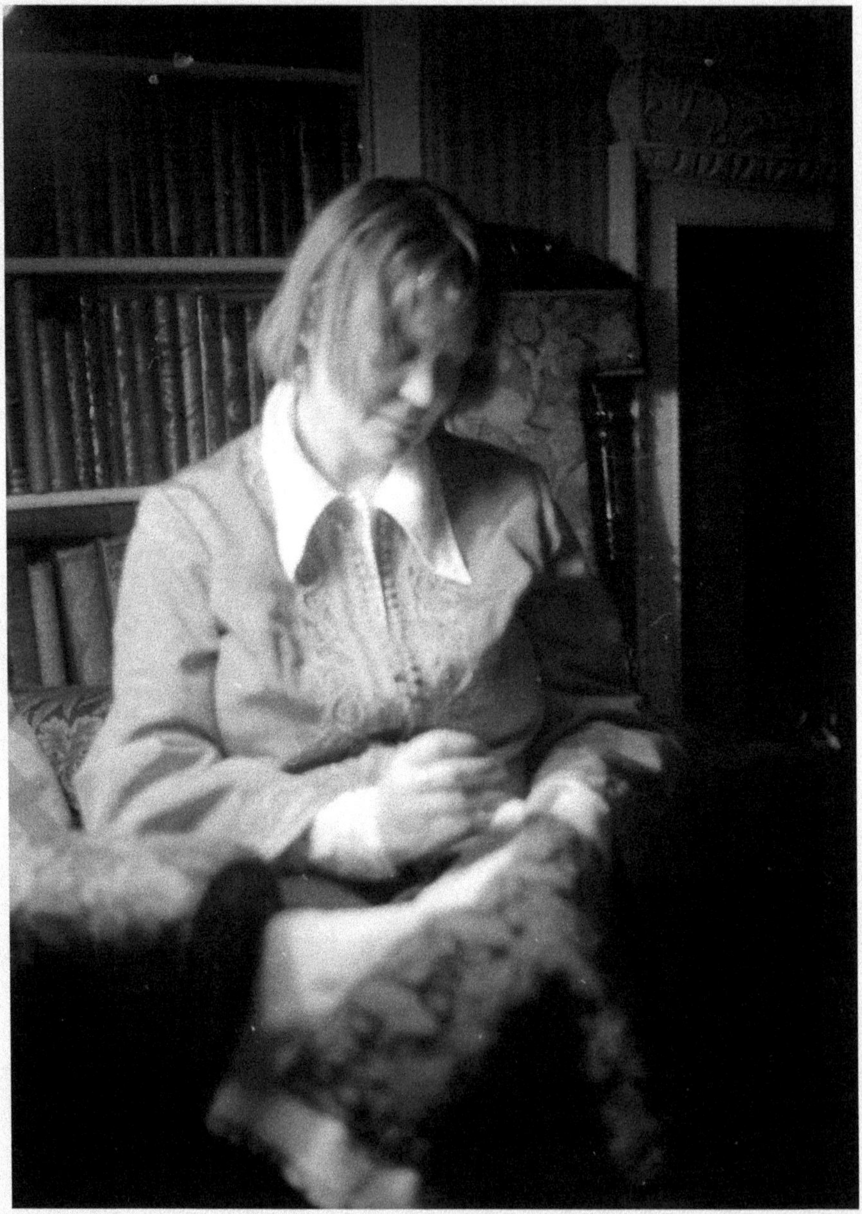

Iris Murdoch as I didn't Know her

A.N. Wilson in Conversation with Miles Leeson

Miles Leeson:
I'm delighted that Andrew is able to join us this afternoon 15 years since he wrote *Iris Murdoch As I Knew Her*. Andrew is of course well known for his work with the BBC, many works of fiction and non-fiction, so it's wonderful that he's with us to talk about Iris Murdoch and his reflections on his biography. Andrew, we welcome you to Chichester, thank you so much for coming. Perhaps that's a good place to start our conversation actually, considering the work. When we were talking a little earlier you said that you hadn't read it for a little while…

A.N. Wilson:
I haven't read it since I wrote it, and I was astonished when I read it last week how indiscreet I've been, but I was quite impressed by some of it though, because I did write down so much. I wish I'd been a kind of Eckerman writing down the conversations of Goethe but if I did have a conversation with her I did tend to write it down and I'm pleased that some of those were in there. But I don't think I was a very good Eckerman and I don't think I asked the right questions; you would've all asked much better questions.

Leeson:
So reflecting on it, and I know you also wrote an article after the death of John Bayley as well reflecting on his work, how do you perceive her now, not just the writing of this work but also back to when you knew her.

Wilson:
Well I think I wanted to write the book because fifteen years ago the picture of her as an Alzheimer's patient was so dominant. The film – if you mentioned her name to people who weren't in a gathering like this but were general readers – they tended to just speak of her as if she

were somebody who suffered from dementia. I wanted to recapture the wonderful original human being who had written these novels which we're all here to celebrate and who had this particular take on philosophy. I know nothing about philosophy but I still like hearing the words of those who do know about philosophy. I mean the mystery is if you've known somebody, and I did know her on one level quite well and on another level I didn't know her at all, but I saw a lot of her. I was taught by her husband John Bayley for three years. If you've known somebody on a pretty frequent basis and if you then read these remarkable books, you do sort of wonder where do they all come from and what is the relationship between the person I knew and the books. And I don't think I've answered that question to my own satisfaction let alone any other readers in this book, but I've tried to, and I think there are preoccupations within the novels. Things which I wish I'd been here earlier that you've been already talking about in relation to gender, trauma, the difficulty of human relationships, the madness, the insanity of falling in love, the damage it does to us, the fact that we're all prone to making crazy emotional adventures and so on, this is what she seems to write about.

Leeson:
In the book you reflect on your readings of the novels and, as you say, there are good elements in almost all of them. I know you're keener on some than others. Has your view of her fiction changed in the last 15 years?

Wison:
Yes, very very much, and one of the things that shocked me about this book was how breezy I was. I do say at the end that I was shocked by my earlier reactions to her asking me, which she did, would I write her biography. I didn't want to write the book and the reason she asked me to write it was that she knew I would never write it. She wanted it to be known that somebody was writing her biography so that nobody else would do it, because she was embarrassed by the prospect. Some publisher in London by the name of Richard Cohen got it into his head that while she was still alive somebody should write her biography. Now, we've all read Peter Conradi's biography and you can see especially why she felt she didn't want this story to be told while her nearest and dearest were still alive. I don't think anybody who knew her on the kind of superficial level I knew her, had any conception of quite what an adventure her life had been, from an emotional point of view. Quite apart from that she was, as most writers are, an instinctively inward, private person so I think the

idea of biography was something that she shied away from and very much disbelieved in. I remember having several conversations with her in which she said she thought, for example, T.S. Eliot was absolutely right to specify there should be no biography written of him and if you want to find out about a writer you read their book, you don't read tittle-tattle about their private life. I think the older I get the more I share that view. But you ask me, have I changed my mind about the novels. Yes, I think the more time recedes the more one sees that a novel like *The Sea, The Sea, The Black Prince*, they're very remarkable books and nobody else wrote books like this. They're not strictly speaking philosophical novels but they are novels in which philosophy and the way we all think about life, and as I say the way we respond to the chaos of being in love or not being in love, they're all explored in the most extraordinary way. And I think her reverence for Shakespeare, which particularly shines out in *The Black Prince*, certainly one of my favourites if not my favourite, has that abundance. She had that imaginative abundance of characters and ideas and conversations and thoughts about life bubbling through her in the most extraordinary prodigious way and that's certainly something which I'm aware of more and more. Many of the works of her contemporaries, however clever they may be, seem a little bit flat to me compared to things she was brave enough to do.

Leeson:
A brave novelist, I think, throughout her career bringing in some of the issues we've been highlighting this weekend…

Wilson:
Obviously there are very few in this room who are old enough to have read them as they came out, these novels, because you're all by my standards amazingly young-looking, but at the time, almost all the novels seemed revolutionary, especially in their approach to the emotional life, to gender, to sexual orientation and so on. I mean when *The Bell* appeared, I was only a little boy but I remember my parents talking about it and speaking about it in absolutely shocked tones, the idea that it might be admitted that members of the Church of England were homosexuals was absolutely horrific to my mother who went to the Early Service every week of her life. Even though everybody 'knew' that the Church of England would collapse if all the gays members were asked to depart. Nonetheless, nobody talked about it and here was a novel exploring the nature of the religious temperament, sexuality, sexual orientation, quite openly and many of the

things in that book which today would seem commonplace to the all the younger members of this audience, they were completely revolutionary.

Leeson:
And being explored to much greater length; certainly when *The Bell* came out it was pre-Wolfenden report…

Wilson:
She was very sound. One of the things I slightly regret about my book is that I do make a slight jibe of her and John Bayley and some of their views. Some of her views, particularly when she was defending Mr Paisley, do strike me as fairly silly I must admit to you, but we're all silly, and one friend when he read this book when it came out 15 years ago quoted the lines by W.H. Auden on Yates, 'You were silly like us, your gift survived it all'. Certainly her gift has survived it all and although I do quote opinions such as her love of Mr Paisley, on the whole I think her opinions have stood the test of time remarkably well. Both her exploration of theology and Plato and the more workaday semi-political questions about whether there should be women priests and that sort of thing; she was a tremendously keen advocate of all that. In one of the biographies, it is probably in Peter Conradi's book, there's a wonderful photograph of her and John Bayley going to a party: he's dressed as the bishop's wife and Iris is dressed as a bishop and they're holding up a banner saying 'Women Bishops Now' which is very characteristic in lots of ways.

Leeson:
So to take you back in time a little bit further than 15 years, you'd been asked to write the biography and then of course ultimately John Bayley asked Peter to write one. What was the moment in your mind when you thought I must also write something now, was it after her death or were the ideas fermenting already?

Wilson:
No, I didn't really want to write it ever. I didn't want to write a formal biography; it's not just that I would have been embarrassed to know the stuff that's in the Peter Conradi biography because you know somebody socially, and particularly if they're older than you are. At one point in the book and I'd forgotten this but the BBC came down and interviewed me and they said, what your relationship with Iris Murdoch, and I said the closest I can get to it is Julie Andrews in *The Sound of Music*, and

the abbess that sings 'Climb Every Mountain'. It was a bit like that, my relationship with her, and she indeed looked rather like the abbess in *The Sound of Music*! She would have made an absolutely top-hole abbess apart from the emotional side of things which might have been slightly chaotic. Because of that being our relationship I would've been far too embarrassed, whether she was dead or alive, to write the book that Peter Conradi had to write. Nowadays biographers, have to tell about love affairs and all the quarrels and that sort of thing, but nonetheless in an infinitely peculiar way I did revere her while also thinking she could be incredibly silly in some of her views. So I wanted to record the actual person I'd known and although I'm mean about John in this book I loved him dearly as well. I wanted to recapture the strange nature of their relationship and how they appeared to people socially because they were adored both in London and in Oxford and they were cherished because they seemed vulnerable; they seemed like Babes in the Wood really. I wanted to capture all of that because I felt the film, brilliantly moving as it was, had taken us away from reality and I wanted to recapture some of the reality. Because it's a chatty, rather lightweight book in many ways – I don't think she was lightweight but I am! – I wanted to capture some of the most ephemeral things of all which was the conversations and what it was like to be with her and what she liked drinking and what her clothes were like and so forth. And one is interested in that, I mean even if you were writing the life of Socrates you would actually be quite interested in knowing what his tastes were if you took him into a restaurant in Athens.

Leeson:
And the tastes were rather diverse and eccentric in some ways, weren't they?

Wilson:
She loved food but never ate properly and it always strikes me now as slightly sad. She always just messed about food, not just with John Bayley's appalling concoctions which nobody actually wanted to eat but if you went to a restaurant she would always be like a child being taken out saying I want to have osso buco, it's my favourite thing, and hardly ever finished it, just pushed it around the plate while she was talking. Partly because she was a very heavy drinker and eating and drinking don't always go together.

Leeson:
You also mentioned earlier in the day some regrets about the book.

Wilson:
I think one regrets hurting other people's feelings. Certainly, I'm 66 now, once you get past the age of 60, you wake up in the middle of the night thinking of all the unnecessary hurt you've caused by one thing or another, and certainly writing this book I now realise caused hurt of that kind. I've been unimaginative when I was writing it. So that one regrets. And I think I regret in a way, although I wanted to write the chatty kind of book I've described, I wish I'd been more seriously engaged; I don't mean the work lacks gaiety and esprit and joy because it's full of it and it's funny too, but she was a totally committed artist. All the reflections she makes in the novels and non-fiction of the later period about the flaying of Marsyas, that myth that meant so much to her, and above all as expressed in the Titian painting, that really was how she conceived an artist's life: that you were flayed, that your skin was removed by the gods.

Leeson:
Would you say that your work was a reaction to Bayley's trilogy?

Wilson:
I slightly petulantly in this book suggest that it was. When I read this book, I hadn't read it for 15 years, I was asking myself what on earth possessed John Bayley, who was such a delightful and amusing man. The first one, the first volume, I think he sort of had to write. Whether he had to publish it, I don't know, because I think if you've been through an awful experience like that, particularly if you are a natural writer as they both were, you do write things down. You write letters to your friends, you write journals and whatever, even so even in that book I felt there were things that shouldn't have been published, they were too humiliating to both of them. The second and third ones I mean we needn't go into it, for a start he admitted that they weren't true and that he'd made things up. And then the film perpetuated a kind of myth really. I mean, I don't sit in judgement because those who care for the mentally ill themselves nearly always suffer some form of mental illness themselves, it's very catching if you're living with someone who isn't linked to reality anymore. To that extent it's a judgemental book and I'm far less judgemental now aged 60 than I was aged 50.

Leeson:
It would have been a different book.

Wilson:
I wouldn't be able to write it now. So to that extent I'm glad I wrote
it because there's quite a lot in there that'd totally forgotten and the
conversations are rather wonderful that she had. I'd love to hear proper
philosophers talking about where she stands over all these great questions
which she and her friends Mary Midgley and Philippa Foot and so on were
brave enough to engage with when a lot of the philosophers at Oxford who
were male felt that chaps don't really talk about all that rubbish; ethics and
religion and so on.

Leeson:
Thinking about her standing now, not only in philosophy but also in
fiction, certainly following her death there was a slump in reputation.
Talking earlier you said returning to the books you'd found so much to
admire there that she is probably in need of re-evaluation by the general
reader.

Wilson:
It would be lovely if some of the shorter earlier books like *The Bell* or *The
Unicorn* which I very much admire could be on an A-level syllabus or
something of that kind. I strongly suspect they will be one day. People's
reputations, particularly those of novelists, seem to slump almost
invariably when they enter old age or die. My wife is re-reading all the
works of Angus Wilson at the moment, no relation of mine, though a great
friend of Iris' incidentally, and reading out bits to me and they reminded
me how absolutely wonderful those novels were. They are almost forgotten
now, and Elizabeth Taylor and Elizabeth Bowen, many of these writers that
we have cherished so much almost sunk without trace in many circles, and
certainly as far as A-level students are concerned. I think that Iris would
be a very good subject for study in schools because there's so much going
on, both the stuff you're discussing at this conference, and the sociological
and the emotional side of things. Going back to what I was saying about
The Bell earlier, and my mother's reaction to it, I think it would be really
interesting to read *The Bell* with a group of 17-year-olds and see what they
thought, both about the reflections on marriage, the reflections on what it
meant to be gay, and all the religious stuff, which is fascinating.

Leeson:
Thinking to your own fictional work, I know you've mention it in the book here, but I wondered if you could say a little bit more about what she meant to you as an artist as you began to practise your craft and can you, at this stage in your life, see the influence more clearly?

Wilson:
I've just finished writing a novel, funnily enough, and when I read the first draft I thought to myself, this is a novel by you, Andrew Wilson, but somebody else has very much been influencing you and I thought it's a kind of Irisy-novel actually. It's about two women who are two New Zealand Anglicans who realise they're in love with one another so it's a very St Anne's, Oxford kind of tale in some ways. I've certainly been influenced by her, both in terms of personal encouragement because most people think it's a good idea just to hone your craft before you dare to pick up your pen or laptop. She was a great one for just diving in and just write and write and write and of course the accusation when you do that is that you're writing too much or that you're being too profuse but I've always followed her in that, and certainly in the actual craft of a novel. In the early days I used to just write books, I now always follow her advice which was personal advice to me which was that you should plot out the whole thing before you even start page one. You should know who all the characters are and where they all end up, even though you might change it as you go along.

Leeson:
And you find that some of the ideas and concerns that influenced her also influence you?

Wilson:
Well they certainly do influence me and she influences me to this day, I'm constantly thinking about what she would've thought about things. As well as being a thinker, she was a great craftsman and when one met her it was a bit like meeting someone who'd just come out of their potter's studio who was still spattered with clay because her hands were nearly always blue with ink! I saw her on Oxford Station catching up, rather like Trollope writing on the railway station, when John Bayley broke his ankle and was taken into hospital and I went to see him. She was sitting at the end of the bed, the pad was still there with the fountain pen going across the page and I think she was writing, rather appropriately given what had just happened

to him, *The Accidental Man*. It certainly was a title which applied to him in many respects, not that it was about him. So she never stopped and she was a real craftswoman and she prided herself on the quality of her prose. I think she was a wonderful prose writer, wonderfully observant, and she loved the music of a sentence and she worked hard. When people said, oh she's just dashed it off, yes she was prolific but she worked hard at those books. And she thought not only about the plot but the whole shape of it. I haven't gone through the archives and things but I bet it would be very interesting to see the extent to which a first draft and second draft were changed and so forth.

Leeson:
How was your relationship with her, if we can talk a little bit about that? Obviously you were taught by John for a few years and then got to meet them, was it a pupil-teacher relationship? She gave you support, encouragement, but the informal friendship grew.

Wilson:
Well we used to see a lot of one another. I got married quite young, so my wife was in the English faculty with John as a teacher at Oxford and we often went to their house in Steeple Aston, I should think once a fortnight for ten years or so. And then I had a sort of particular friendship with John and used to go and see him at St Cat's where he taught by then. We'd have lunch and then walk round the meadow together. And then, little by little, it was long before any idea of my writing about her occurred, I was moving more in London direction, and she suggested that we meet. My sister had a flat very near her flat and my sister liked going to Iris' favourite restaurant which was called Deano's in Gloucester Road. She didn't like posh restaurants and she didn't like good wine, she always said you mustn't allow your palate to become used to good wine, you must live on plonk because otherwise you'll never drink enough basically. And I remember having a lovely lunch with her at Deano's and obviously pushing the food around the plate and I said to Rachel Tricket who was the friend of John Bayley and Iris' that I'd had this nice lunch with Iris and she said, without John? And I said yes, without John. And she said that will mean the end of your friendship with John Bayley. I thought this was utter fantasy but it was only after about two years had passed that I realised my little lunches with John never happened again after that. And there are several other examples of it which I'd completely forgotten. They were very close to a person called John Jones who was the professor of poetry

at Oxford and Iris met Mrs John Jones who was called Jean Robertson at Cambridge during her year in Cambridge when she met all the disciples of Wittgenstein. Jean once said to Iris, it was after Iris had left St Anne's and she had this routine of coming up to Oxford from London, having done her teaching at the Royal College, and then she would meet John Jones who was, although he was the English don he was very interested in philosophy, and they met in a pub called the Roebuck and they drank a couple of pints of beer and then had chasers, vodka chasers, and then they went their separate ways. When Jean Jones said this to John and Iris, John looked appalled and it never happened again, Iris never had her tête-a-tête with Jones. So whatever was going on behind the apparently very jolly surface of things John was clearly very jealous and possessive of her in relation to his own friends. She had hundreds of friends of course, and I was completely unaware of all that, so in the last 10 or 15 years, we saw them as a group, married couples together having supper. But with her, particularly when she dropped this idea that I should write the book, she did see me *à deux* a lot, and I'll just read you one bit of the book which in a way is my favourite bit of the book. I'd completely forgotten this, it's not me, it's at the beginning, I'd been to Reading University to look at the archives of Chatto & Windus, and here's a memo from the Iris' publisher at Chatto & Windus, Carmen Callil, 1989. 'Could you go through Iris' files and reviews and look up names of people who could do a major interview of her for Arena (which must be some television programme I think)? Ed Victor has suggested A.N. Wilson to her, but Alan Yentob isn't keen – too alienating.' In fact we did make that programme and she took it terribly seriously of course, because I think she began to realise that although there had been programmes made about her before that, it was inevitable that the story of her life was going to be told. She told quite a lot about her life in that programme actually, in an oblique kind of way.

Leeson:
The publication of the Conradi biography was a revelation and in some respects a shock then…

Wilson:
I think it was a shock to everybody. I still haven't quite, I don't mean in moral terms, I mean in terms of assessing how she spent her time, how she had time to have all these love affairs and write all these books, I mean the energy is prodigious. But I mean it is true but people of huge creativity, I mean we've already mentioned Eckerman; Goethe was far more energetic

than many other people. And Iris was a person of phenomenal strength, I mean when you saw her swimming – the film starts with her swimming but that was when she was old and ill – she was a very powerful swimmer. She was very gymnastic and John Bayley's first vision of her was seeing her whizz past on a bicycle which is rather like a John Betjeman poem, but you know she was sporty. She loved all the sport like badminton and she had tremendous energy. Obviously she had great intellectual energy, that goes without saying.

One of the things which happened to me while I was reading this book last week, and thinking back, was asking myself the inevitable question you do ask yourself when someone's developed that particular type of illness of, when did she start to unravel? You start to think, well had it all begun much earlier? I can remember the awful year in which she gave the Gifford lectures in Scotland and she was separated from John. John couldn't do the journey to Scotland; he couldn't travel on public transport basically, he was frightened of it and there was a terrible day he got lost in Birmingham changing trains. He got off the train because somebody tried to engage him in conversation and said 'What do you do?' and John didn't want to say what he did, perhaps he didn't know what he did. The man said well don't tell me, I think you're a lawyer, and John said 'Sort of' and got off the train having no idea where it was, and Iris was waiting in Aberdeen or Edinburgh or wherever it was that the Giffords were happening that year in terrible distress. While all that was happening their garden got trashed by some village children and Iris sort of lost it at that point, she was terribly unhappy, she felt the world was ganging up against them, and she also genuinely shocked that the lectures went down terribly badly in Scotland, they were not well received. I think she thought that they were going to be well received, and I mean it's quite a task, it's not just 8 lectures; and she felt she had to go back and do her homework more for them, and in particular her engagement with Heidegger. I don't say it sent her round the bend but anyone who's been brave enough to read through *Sein und Zeit* is likely to have a slightly confused take on the world because you must wonder if your head's spinning round, I've only read half of it. At this point John made this impulsive decision to sell their house and buy a tiny house in Oxford Street so there was no room for her to work or anything, and she started writing and writing that book over and over again. She just couldn't get it into focus, she didn't dare to publish the lectures as they'd been given because they'd gone down so badly, and that was the time when I was seeing a lot of her. It was also the time, thinking of an earlier question, when the idea of a dialogue came to pass and I think it would've been wonderful if I'd had been a proper philosopher and she'd actually done the book as dialogues possibly, perhaps with some invented characters. I don't know now if I would say that *Metaphysics as a Guide to Morals* destroyed the art, I wouldn't say that, but undoubtedly the personal distress of that year and the obsession with trying to get Heidegger and Wittgenstein out of her system or into her philosophical mode of thinking, and I speak as an absolute non-philosopher, did send her off the rails somewhat. I'm not saying it contributed to her illness because it was way before then but it caused a crisis in the writing.

Leeson:
You said you might originally write the biography as a dialogue between you and Iris Murdoch.

Wilson:
Well I'm glad you asked that question because the only moment when the idea of my writing about her became serious between the two of us, we followed that up and we actually had a go at it but it didn't work. I don't think, and this isn't false modesty, I wasn't clever enough to do it. In order to be able to do it you would have had to be Plato to her Socrates, you would have had to be able to keep up with what she was trying to say about Immanuel Kant for example. I could do it with Plato because I have read the Dialogues of Plato quite often but I've never really come to terms with *The Critique of Pure Reason* and I think it would've come unstuck. But she certainly wanted to do that. It would be fascinating if one had got her to speak about her life not merely as a member of the Communist Party but as somebody who in a very minor way was involved in politics in London. I also think her relationship to theology, and her attempts to expound a take on the Christian religion which removed the personal god, are still very interesting ones. And I think there will be lots of room there for somebody deeper and cleverer than myself to explore, and precisely in that form, and also I think, I quote little bits here when she was talking about friends being important to her, whether they were lovers or simply friends, I think that's also a very good way of doing a biography. When you read Eckerman's conversations with Goethe, his conversations about Schiller in particular, I think that to have Iris talking in a slightly more candid way than she was ever prepared to do with me, for example her relationship with Raymond Queneau, her feelings about Sartre, her relationships with Brigid Brophy. I mean what's interesting about her

relationship with Brigid Brophy isn't so much that they were lovers but all the literary stuff they had in common, and then stuff they didn't have in common and the rows they had, I mean all that's utterly fascinating. So that's rather too long an answer but I think it could've been done and it's too late now but I think one should always bear it in mind if one meets a great person that that is actually the way to do it. Nietzsche always used to say that the greatest book written in German was the conversations with Goethe and I think he was right really. I hardly need to say it in this company, but Plato knew a thing or two about how to do this. I think Iris' own Platonic dialogues are wonderful.

Leeson:
Could you say more about her being an observer of ordinary life?

Wilson:
When I was talking about her being an observer of the London scene I meant her being an observer of what was going on inside people and the emotional transformations. This involved the sexual revolution, the Church of England, and indeed other bodies but particularly the Church of England coming to terms with religious unbelief, the whole Death of God movement and everything else. As a social observer she gave up probably in about 1956 at noticing what the real world was like and I remember her saying to me in all seriousness in about 1980, somebody had mentioned the *Daily Mail* and she paused and said 'I don't think I like that newspaper' and well, all intelligent people always say that whether they read it or not, and I realised and I said 'Why not?' and she said 'Well, isn't it very left-wing?'. I doubt she'd ever read a copy of that newspaper or even seen one probably. I remember one of the people at Chatto saying to me, because she had this thing of refusing to change anything towards the end, and they pointed out to her there was some detail on the London transport system, it was either a bus that didn't go to a particular place or an underground station that had closed before the war or something, she just wouldn't alter it and as far as she was concerned that was the world and I mean it is Murdochland, her books, it isn't describing contemporary Britain in any sense, she despised contemporary culture. She had no idea, she used to say one of the reasons – this is what I mean about distinguishing the wise woman from the woman who basically hadn't observed anything for 40 years – I remember her saying to me, I mean long before she was ill or anything, that she thought the soap opera was one of the reason why public morals and everything else had collapsed. I said well which ones,

well they're all terrible but she had no idea what a modern soap opera was, I think she thought it was a kind of modern Gilbert & Sullivan, I honestly think she thought it had musical accompaniment. She followed the Beatles. She loved the Beatles and knew most of their songs by heart, but I think that was the end of any engagement she had with popular culture.

Leeson:
There's a common view which I think you share in your book that the earlier novels were in fact better than the later novels and she reached her climax in *The Sea, The Sea* and then sort of went off and became all eccentric. Do you still agree with that view or do you agree with Murdoch scholars who are every year building up the reputation of these later novels?

Wilson:
Well, I have to admit to you I haven't read *The Message to the Planet* for example since it came out. I suspect that when I read the later books again I will move more in the direction you're suggesting. I love some of the early novels, I love *The Flight from the Enchanter* and so forth but of course they're not in the same league as *The Sea, The Sea*. And what's so exciting about this trajectory is that she's moving all the time, isn't she. So I strongly suspect that if I start at the beginning and worked my way through to the end I would start to see all sorts of things, in *The Green Knight* for example. I mean, they are very long aren't they? And they are very profuse. And perhaps repetitive, I don't know. Not that that's necessarily a fault.
The publishers used to regard them with absolute dread when they arrived, the size of the parcel that she was just about strong enough to carry into the offices at Chatto filled them with absolute horror, and by then the sales had started to drop. Certainly up to *The Book and the Brotherhood*. I love *The Book and the Brotherhood* but I do long for… this is meant to be a book about a man who's in a way writing a great Marxist synthesis but you never get any sense of him relating to real political events, what's happening in the Soviet Union, what's happening in the Middle East, nothing, it just relates to Murdochland, and it seems really strange that somebody can be as left-wing as everybody's meant to be in *The Book and the Brotherhood* and not be engaged in the actual world which is the world of all of us, as Wordsworth calls it.

Leeson:
It's interesting that John gives up writing fiction quite early on in their marriage, and then picks up fictional writing again in the 1980s. What do you think their literary relationship was like?

Wilson:
It's a difficult question to answer coherently so I'll have to given an incoherent answer. She certainly revered John as a critic and she saw him as in the tradition of Matthew Arnold. There's a bit at the beginning – this isn't quite an answer but it's a sort of answer – if you remember when he's about to fall in love with Julian in *The Black Prince*, Bradley Pearson is asked by Julian who says she wants to be a writer what she should do. He replies 'You should read *The Iliad* and then you should read all the great authors of the 19th century, particularly the English and the Russians' and she did do that all the time and one of the things she had in common with John Bayley was that he did that all the time too. Going back to the question we were talking about earlier and the fact that Murdochland seems to have less and less to do with England in the '60s, '70s, '80s, is that she was really just as happy in the London of Dickens, or the St Petersburg of Dostoyevsky, as she was in her own contemporary world. Nevertheless, one of things that she wanted to be was not just a popular 20th-century novelist, she wanted to write in the great tradition of the novelists she revered, and whenever she was writing a book I always feel there's one of these giants sort of hovering around her. I think Hartley in *The Sea, The Sea* is close to Proust. I mean it's totally different to Proust but her reading of Proust over and over again was something that formed an enormous part of her life and similarly with Dostoyevsky novels, she read the four main ones endless numbers of times. I'm sorry that's not really an answer but it's a sort of answer and it's certainly something she and John had together.

Leeson:
And the title of the work, *Iris Murdoch: As I Knew Her* – do you still believe that?

Wilson:
I think if I reissued this book I think I would retitle it *Iris Murdoch as I Did Not Know Her*. I think she remained a complete mystery certainly to me, and even just this afternoon talking about her I realise how little I knew her. I think not in any relation to her, but in relation to other writers

I've either read about or known in person, one of the things that goes on, particularly with creative writers, poets, playwrights and novelists, is that presumably the bits of their incoherent personality find coherent form in the art. I think I find that absolutely triumphantly in *The Black Prince* – her thoughts about literature, her dread of what started when she began becoming such a fluent writer. She's seeing herself as Bradley Pearson sees Arnold Baffin with his almost ridiculous profusion and his capacity to write in a way quite trashy love stories but weaves them in and out of thoughts about Christ and everything else. I mean nobody's said anything harsher about Iris Murdoch's novels than Bradley Pearson says about Arnold Baffin's, and yet you feel there both the emotional chaos that appears in the letters and the biography being contained in the most extraordinary way and related to the philosophy and so on. I don't think it's realistic to expect any human being to be coherent and we don't know one another. I mean we don't know ourselves, and that's why personal relationships are so difficult because the other person sees a whole lot of truth about us which we would be in complete denial about until we decided to spend a lot of time with them and they suddenly see a figure that we hardly knew, one we didn't know at all.

Leeson:
To conclude our talk together this afternoon, your lasting impression of her now, is it as an artist, as a friend?

Wilson:
I love her as an artist and I'm really grateful when I look at my bookshelves; they're friends, these books, I love reading them because it's not like talking to her but there's a voice there which is so distinctive and the stories and characters and the situations they're in. All those reflections on Shakespeare in *The Black Prince* for example, and so that's one thing for which I'm incredibly grateful. But I do think of her as one of the wise women of our times and I think the fact that I now realise, having got over the surprise of the Peter Conradi book, is that the emotional chaos in which she lived is made into art in all the books. I used to think of her books that people can't fall in love with 17 different people with all these permutations but then you realise, well, actually the author could, and perhaps that is what the 1950s and '60s and '70s to a smaller extent were a bit like. There was this extraordinary revolution going on, emotional, moral, ethical, political, social, while she was writing and although she wasn't interested in the technical side of politics she was describing the

modern world to itself in the most extraordinary way and I think *au fond* she was a very wise person. I think in a way her take on the importance of the inner life, the importance of the spiritual life both in one's art and in one's day-to-day life is something that she spoke up for above all in *The Sovereignty of Good* which I think is one of her absolute masterpieces of and indeed of anybody's writing in my lifetime. I think we can all look back on that with tremendous gratitude.

Contributors

Audi Bayley (1942 -)
Close friend of Iris Murdoch and John Bayley for over thirty years and widow of John Bayley whom she married in 2000.

Cheryl Bove (1944 -)
American editor of the *Iris Murdoch News Letter* from 1998-2007 and editor of the IMNL from 1995-1998. Her publications include: *Sacred Space, Beloved City: Iris Murdoch's London* (2008), co-authored with Anne Rowe; *Iris Murdoch: A Descriptive Primary and Annotated Secondary Bibliography*, co-authored with John Fletcher (1994); *Understanding Iris Murdoch* (1993) and *A Character Index and Guide to the Fiction of Iris Murdoch* (1986).

Marjorie Boulton (1924 - 2017)
Author, poet, teacher and expert in Esperanto. A lifelong friend of Iris Murdoch whom she met on going up to Somerville College, Oxford, in 1941.

Dame Carmen Callil (1938 -)
Best known as a publisher, she founded the Virago Press in 1972. She has also written a number of books in her own right.

Eric Christiansen (1937 - 2016)
History fellow at New College Oxford and reviewer for academic journals and magazines including the *Spectator* and the *New York Review of Books*.

Dame Philippa Foot (1920 - 2010)
Philosopher and author who held visiting professorships at Cornell, MIT, UCLA, Berkeley and the City University of New York before settling at the University of California in Los Angeles in 1976 where she became Griffin

Professor of Philosophy in 1988. Author of a number of philosophical works including *Virtues and Vices* (1978) and *Natural Goodness* (2001).

John Grigg (1924 - 2001)
Writer, historian and politician. He was the Second Baron Altrincham from 1955 until he disclaimed that title under the Peerage Act on the day it received the Royal Assent in 1963.

Josephine Hart, Lady Saatchi (1942 - 2011)
Irish novelist, theatrical producer, television presenter and founder of Gallery Poets. She ran the Josephine Hart Poetry Hour at various locations in the West End and organised highly successful poetry readings at the British Library. Her novel, *Damage*, was made into a film starring Juliette Binoche, Jeremy Irons and Rupert Graves.

Roy Jenkins, Lord Jenkins of Hillhead (1920 - 2003)
British politician who was a Labour MP who served as Home Secretary, Chancellor of the Exchequer and Deputy Head of the Labour Party. He became President of the European Commission and went on to found the Social Democrat Party (SDP). He was made a life peer in 1987, and became Chancellor of Oxford University until his death. He wrote best-selling biographies of Gladstone and Churchill.

Kate Levey (1957 -)
The daughter of the novelist Brigid Brophy and former director of the National Gallery, Michael Levey.

Paul Levy FRSL (1941 -)
The food and wine editor of *The Observer* (1980-91); European cultural correspondent, *The Wall Street Journal* (1991-2015) and a frequent broadcaster. His books ranging from *G.E.Moore & The Cambridge Apostles* to *Out to Lunch*. He is the literary executor of the Strachey Trust and Chair Emeritus, Oxford Food Symposium.

Miles Leeson (1981 -)
Director of the Iris Murdoch Research Centre at the University of Chichester, and the author of *Iris Murdoch: Philosophical Novelist* (2010).

Ben MacIntyre (1963 -)
British author, historian, reviewer and columnist writing for *The Times*.
His columns range from current affairs to historical controversies.

Tom Phillips CBE, RA (1937 -)
English painter, printmaker and collagist. An establishment figure in most
aspects of the arts. He has been a trustee of the National Portrait Gallery,
an Honorary Fellow of the London Institute, an Honorary Member of the
Royal Society of Portrait Painters and a Trustee of the British Museum.

Suguna Ramanathan (1940 -)
Retired head of the English Department and dean of the arts faculty at St
Xavier's College, Ahmedabad, India. Author of *Iris Murdoch: Figures of
Good* (1990.)

Father Pierre Riches (1921 - 2019)
An Italian-speaking Jewish Alexandrian. A theologian and author of three
books on Roman Catholicism in today's society.

Lady Natasha Spender (1919 - 2010)
Pianist, author and gardener, she became a specialist in the psychology
of music. Wife of the poet, novelist and essayist Sir Stephen Spender, she
wrote a book about her late husband and her passion for gardening at their
home, Mas Saint Jerome, in Provence, *An English Garden in Provence* in
1988. Her book *An English Country Garden* was published in 2004.

Miklos Veto (1936 -)
A Hungarian-born French philosopher. He studied for his DPhil under
Murdoch at Oxford, which became *The Religious Metaphysics of Simone
Weil*. He became a world expert in German idealism, especially Schelling,
and continues to write. He lives in Paris.

A. N. Wilson (1950 -)
One of Britain's leading novelists and non-fiction writers. He has written
biographies of, among others, Jesus, Dante, Darwin, Tolstoy, St. Paul, and
Iris Murdoch.

Lightning Source UK Ltd.
Milton Keynes UK
UKHW021441050221
378267UK00001B/5/J

9 781912 972005